MAKING TIME FOR
SOCIAL STUDIES

A Four-Step Process for Unit Planning in the Elementary Classroom

RACHEL SWEARENGIN

Solution Tree | Press
a division of
Solution Tree

555 North Morton Street
Bloomington, IN 47404
800.733.6786 (toll free) / 812.336.7700
FAX: 812.336.7790

email: info@SolutionTree.com
SolutionTree.com

Visit **go.SolutionTree.com/instruction** to download the free reproducibles in this book.

Printed in the United States of America

Library of Congress Cataloging-in-Publication Data

Names: Swearengin, Rachel, author.
Title: Making time for social studies : a four-step process for unit
   planning in the elementary classroom / Rachel Swearengin.
Description: Bloomington, IN : Solution Tree Press, 2025. | Includes
   bibliographical references and index.
Identifiers: LCCN 2024034284 (print) | LCCN 2024034285 (ebook) | ISBN
   9781960574947 (paperback) | ISBN 9781960574954 (ebook)
Subjects: LCSH: Social sciences--Study and teaching (Elementary)--United
   States. | Social sciences--Study and teaching
   (Elementary)--Curricula--United States. | Curriculum planning--United
   States.
Classification: LCC LB1584 .S936 2025 (print) | LCC LB1584 (ebook) | DDC
   372.890973--dc23/eng/20240826
LC record available at https://lccn.loc.gov/2024034284
LC ebook record available at https://lccn.loc.gov/2024034285

Solution Tree
Jeffrey C. Jones, CEO
Edmund M. Ackerman, President

Solution Tree Press
President and Publisher: Douglas M. Rife
Associate Publishers: Todd Brakke and Kendra Slayton
Editorial Director: Laurel Hecker
Art Director: Rian Anderson
Copy Chief: Jessi Finn
Production Editor: Madonna Evans
Copy Editor: Jessica Starr
Proofreader: Elijah Oates
Text and Cover Designer: Laura Cox
Acquisitions Editors: Carol Collins and Hilary Goff
Content Development Specialist: Amy Rubenstein
Associate Editors: Sarah Ludwig and Elijah Oates
Editorial Assistant: Madison Chartier

Acknowledgments

Thank you to my number one supporter, my husband Nathan. You have self-lessly encouraged me to do *all* the things I want to do—even something crazy like writing a book! I love you.

Thank you to my children, Tyler, Julia, and Luke. Being your mother is my greatest joy, and I could not be prouder of each of you. You all teach me something new every day. I love you.

Thank you to my mom and dad, Nelda and Allen. You modeled and taught me the value of hard work growing up, and have always encouraged me to accomplish my dreams. Love you!

Thank you to my sister, Melissa. You were my first "co-teacher" in our basement school room and my first best friend. Your constant support and encouragement mean the world to me. Love you!

To my sister, Stephanie. I know you are smiling down from heaven. I love and miss you every day.

To the many people who have had an impact on my teaching and learning journey—administrators, instructional coaches, content coordinators, teachers, and colleagues—there are too many of you to name, but you know who you are. Thank you for investing your time to teach, encourage, and inspire me to be the best teacher I can be. And a special shout-out to the many educators I have had the privilege to work with at the Kansas State Department of Education—your love and dedication to social studies inspires me every time I'm with you.

Thank you to Solution Tree for giving me the opportunity to try something new. Elijah Oates—thank you for planting the seed that I could write a book. Amy Rubenstein and Madonna Evans—thank you for helping this first-time author turn her ideas into a book that teachers can use. I am forever grateful!

Proverbs 3:5–6 says "Trust in the LORD with all thine heart; and lean not unto thine own understanding. In all thy ways acknowledge him, and he shall direct thy paths (King James Version)." I am so blessed and thankful for each of the people that God has brought into my path and for the special calling He drew me toward when He gave me a passion for teaching.

Solution Tree Press would like to thank the following reviewers:

Molly Capps
Principal
McDeeds Creek Elementary School
Southern Pines, North Carolina

Janet Gilbert
Principal
Mountain Shadows
  Elementary School
Glendale, Arizona

Erin Kruckenberg
Fifth-Grade Teacher
Jefferson Elementary School
Harvard, Illinois

Nathan McAlister
Humanities Program Manager—
  History, Government, and
  Social Studies
Kansas State Department of
  Education
Topeka, Kansas

Sheryl Walters
Senior School Assistant Principal
Calgary, Alberta, Canada

Visit **go.SolutionTree.com/instruction** to download the free reproducibles in this book.

Table of Contents

Reproducibles are in italics.

About the Author

Rachel Swearengin is a fifth-grade teacher for Olathe Public Schools in Kansas. Swearengin has taught kindergarten in addition to fifth grade during her fifteen-year career. Her educational experiences include serving on district standards and curriculum adoption committees, providing both building- and district-level professional development, serving as chair for her building leadership team, serving as a master teacher for new educators in her district, and facilitating sessions at her local EdCamp. She currently serves as a field educator for the humanities department of the Kansas State Department of Education, where she facilitates professional development and serves on assessment and planning committees. She also teaches an elementary social studies methods undergraduate course for Emporia State University in Kansas.

Swearengin is a member of the National Council for the Social Studies, and she has presented at the association's national conference on inquiry in the elementary classroom. Swearengin is passionate about teaching effective social studies in the elementary classroom to prepare even the youngest learners for their roles as productive citizens in a democracy. She is the 2023 recipient of the Gilder Lehrman Institute of American History State History Teacher of the Year award, as well as one of the top ten finalists for the 2023 Gilder Lehrman Institute of American History National History Teacher of the Year award.

Swearengin received a bachelor's degree in elementary education from MidAmerica Nazarene University and a master's degree in curriculum and instruction from Emporia State University.

To learn more about Rachel's work, follow her @rachelteachkc on X.

To book Rachel Swearengin for professional development, contact pd@ SolutionTree.com.

Introduction

Imagine you are a parent in your school community, and you have the opportunity to observe two elementary classes during their respective social studies lessons. You begin by entering classroom A, where students sit quietly at their desks and work independently, their textbooks open as they tackle a worksheet. The teacher explains to you that the students are reading and answering questions concerning the facts and dates of a historical event. After a few minutes, the teacher instructs the students to finish and turn in their papers because it is time to move on to the next subject.

Now imagine walking next door to classroom B. Entering, you direct your attention to a few students at the front of the room who are pointing and talking in raised, excited voices.

"What is that?"

"Where did it come from?"

"What does it mean?"

At that moment, you notice yellow crime scene tape marking off a collection of artifacts from the past. You turn to another group and see students using magnifying glasses to closely study black-and-white photographs before recording their observations—the teacher explains that these are their attempts to tell the story of what's happening in the photographs. Suddenly the teacher tries to get the students' attention, which is rather difficult as they are so deeply engaged in their activities. Finally, she says, "Based on what you have observed and learned so far, can one person change the world?" After a few moments of silence, discussion again fills the room as students articulate their responses to that compelling question and defend their claims with evidence from the many sources they have just analyzed.

Consider which classroom you would want your child to be in: classroom A, where students are reading difficult text on their own and memorizing facts and dates? Or classroom B, where students are using historical thinking to answer an enduring question that leads to further understanding beyond the classroom walls? Of course, parents and teachers alike want classroom B. But as heartening as this classroom is to imagine, elementary educators know firsthand the challenges inherent in bringing it to life. This book offers teachers a resource for preparing the critical types of lessons found in classroom B. In the following pages, let us first explore the need for increased teaching and learning time in social studies before diving into the four-step planning process around which the book is based. From there, we will look at what you can expect from each chapter, along with other book features.

We Need More Teaching and Learning Time in Social Studies

In response to the 2010 release of more rigorous standards in English language arts (ELA) and mathematics as part of the Common Core State Standards, the National Council for the Social Studies (NCSS) in 2013 released *The College, Career, and Civic Life (C3) Framework for Social Studies State Standards: Guidance for Enhancing the Rigor of K–12 Civics, Economics, Geography, and History*. This is commonly referenced as the C3 Framework. With this document, the association intended to provide guidance for U.S. states as they began improving social studies education by increasing the rigor of standards (NCSS, 2013). The C3 Framework not only sought to prepare students for college and career, like the ELA and mathematics standards were doing, but also included a third element: preparation for civic life. In the document's introduction, the writers highlight their motivation for the text—or the beliefs they and all "advocates of citizenship education" share—that "our democratic republic will not sustain unless students are aware of their changing cultural and physical environments; know the past; read, write, and think deeply; and act in ways that promote the common good" (NCSS, 2013, p. 5). Unfortunately, research from a decade on shows that as the emphasis on ELA and mathematics remains strong, social studies instruction often falls by the wayside, with data and literature conveying that students need what the C3 Framework lays out (Carrillo, 2023; Council of Chief State School Officers, 2018; Diliberti, Woo, & Kaufman 2023; Haass

2023; Tyner and Kabourek 2020; Wexler 2019). The development of the C3 Framework implies that civic education should be a part of every student's educational day, from kindergarten through twelfth grade, just as ELA and mathematics instruction are. But is civic education occurring in classrooms?

In *Becoming Active Citizens: Practices to Engage Students in Civic Education Across the Curriculum*, authors Tom Driscoll and Shawn W. McCusker (2022) discuss *civic education* as the Annenberg Classroom (n.d.) defines it: "Teaching the knowledge, skills, and virtues needed for competent citizenship in a democracy." Driscoll and McCusker (2022) clarify that civic education in this way equips students with what they need to both live in and preserve a democracy. Unfortunately, assessments don't provide evidence that students are learning these skills. In the United States, the National Assessment of Educational Progress (NAEP)—often referred to as the Nation's Report Card and administered every four years—assesses what students in public and private schools know and can do in mathematics, reading, science, social studies, and other subjects (National Center for Education Statistics, n.d.). The results for eighth graders from the 2022 NAEP for history and civics show that only 14 percent of students reached the proficient mark or above in history, and only 22 percent of students reached the proficient mark or above in civics. This is a continued downward trend that began in 2014 (Carrillo, 2023).

The decrease in time allotted to social studies instruction in the elementary school classroom has been associated with this decline. This decrease in social studies instruction has occurred as an increase in instructional minutes for ELA and mathematics has occurred. According to a study by researchers Adam Tyner and Sarah Kabourek (2020), "ELA instruction accounts for 39 percent of instructional time in U.S. elementary schools . . . . Science and social studies each occupy about 10 percent" (p. 17). Because of high-stakes testing, instructional time allotments often focus more on subjects like ELA and mathematics and less on subjects like social studies and science. The study went on to say that even in kindergarten through grade 2, where state testing isn't occurring, twenty-five minutes or less is spent on social studies each day (Tyner & Kabourek, 2020).

There are other reasons why social studies receives so little time in the elementary classroom. In reporting the findings of the 2022 American Instructional Resources Survey, researchers Melissa K. Diliberti, Ashley Woo, and Julia H. Kaufman (2023) note that elementary teachers often don't receive professional development related to social studies instruction like they do in mathematics,

ELA, or science. The survey also finds that many elementary teachers don't have access to effective, district-adopted social studies resources, so they are forced to find their own, on their own time (Diliberti et al., 2023). And for other teachers, they simply can't fit it all in, so they drop social studies to teach the required minutes of ELA and mathematics.

The C3 Framework offers a solution for increasing civic education in elementary classrooms: using *inquiry*. Writing for the NCSS, Scott M. Waring (2023) states, "Inquiry consists of exploration through the analysis of sources to answer questions" (p. 5). The C3 Framework then outlines four dimensions necessary for inquiry in social studies (NCSS, 2013).

1. Developing questions and planning inquiries

2. Applying disciplinary concepts and tools

3. Evaluating sources and using evidence

4. Communicating conclusions and taking informed action

Dimension two also includes four subsections: (1) civics, (2) economics, (3) geography, and (4) history. Each subsection includes a description of the structure and the tools needed within that discipline. Table I.1 summarizes the skills and processes within each discipline, according to the C3 Framework (NCSS, 2013).

Table I.1: Four Disciplines of the C3 Framework

Civics	Civic and political institutions; applying civic virtues and democratic principles; processes, rules, and laws
Economics	Economic decision making; exchange and markets; the national economy; the global economy
Geography	Spatial view of the world through geographic representations; human-environment interactions of place, regions, and culture; spatial patterns and movements of human populations; changing spatial patterns through global interconnections
History	Change, continuity, and context; perspectives; historical sources and evidence; causation and argumentation

Source: Adapted from NCSS, 2013.

Since the writers of the C3 Framework called for inquiry as an effective strategy for teaching the framework, teachers next needed an inquiry planning process that incorporated the four dimensions (NCSS, 2013). In response, the lead writers of the C3 Framework, Kathy Swan, John K. Lee, and S. G. Grant (2018), created a three-phase model for teachers to use as they developed inquiries, called the Inquiry Design Model. The three phases of the model are as follows (Swan et al., 2018).

1. Framing the inquiry by identifying content through standards, writing a compelling question, and stress-testing the compelling question by creating a summative performance task

2. Filling the inquiry by writing supporting questions, choosing sources, and developing formative performance tasks

3. Finishing the inquiry by staging the compelling question, identifying extension tasks, and identifying ways to take informed action

The C3 Framework, along with the Inquiry Design Model, provides teachers with a starting point for effective social studies instruction. The four-step planning process outlined in this book helps teachers close the gap between understanding the beliefs and goals of the C3 Framework and Inquiry Design Model and the practical implementation of planning and teaching social studies in the elementary classroom.

The Four-Step Planning Process

A body of research tells us we're not meeting our goal of student success in civic education, but that research doesn't tell us how to change our practice (Carrillo, 2023; Council of Chief State School Officers, 2018; Diliberti, Woo, & Kaufman, 2023; Haass, 2023; Tyner & Kabourek, 2020; Wexler, 2019). This book presents an easy four-step process for planning social studies units to help teachers provide civic education to elementary learners. This process is aligned with the beliefs and goals of the C3 Framework, as well as the inquiry process used in the Inquiry Design Model. The steps of the process are as follows.

1. **Making meaning of social studies standards:** Identify and unpack the social studies standards you want to address in the unit.

2. **Creating assessments:** Create an assessment and plan for informed action so that students not only learn but also *do* social studies.

3. **Choosing and analyzing primary sources:** Choose primary sources to expose students to evidence from civics, economics, geography, or history. Teach students strategies to analyze primary sources.

4. **Choosing and analyzing secondary sources:** Choose secondary sources to expose students to evidence from civics, economics, geography, or history. Teach students strategies to analyze secondary sources.

Note that because this four-step process is for unit planning rather than daily lesson planning, it does not outline step-by-step what you will say and do while teaching—it addresses the important components you need to include in your unit plans. How you use the components in your daily lessons is the art of teaching specific to you as the educator.

A planning template is provided for you to complete as you work through each step of the process. The template is shown in figure I.1. A reproducible version can also be found in appendix A (page 127).

Topic or Unit:	
Step 1: Making Meaning of Standards	
Standard:	
Enduring Understanding:	
Compelling Question:	
Step 2: Creating Assessments	
Classroom-Based Assessment:	
Doing Social Studies:	
Step 3: Choosing and Analyzing Primary Sources	
Step 4: Choosing and Analyzing Secondary Sources	

Figure I.1: The four-step planning process template.

The four-step planning process can be used to plan units of various lengths. You may want to create a two- or three-day unit focused on a single topic or create a two- or three-week unit on multiple topics. For example, you may spend only a day or two on one person's significant contributions to a historical period or spend several weeks teaching about multiple peoples' contributions. The process is the same either way.

One important caveat, however, is that this process assumes that you have instructional time allotted specifically for social studies. This is critical because the literacy skills we use in social studies are different from those used in ELA.

These skills are what we call disciplinary literacy skills. *Disciplinary literacy*, according to the Colorado Department of Education (2020), is "the intersection of content knowledge, experiences, and skills necessary to demonstrate understanding through the ability to read, write, communicate, and think critically using approaches unique to a specific discipline." For example, we don't want to just teach students about history; we want them to think like historians. We want them to read, write, communicate, and think in the same ways as historians.

The same is true for the other discipline-specific lenses of the C3 Framework—we want students to think like economists and geographers. How do we do this? By teaching skills specific to social studies. Educator Joe Schmidt (2022) captures such disciplinary skills in his list of practices "to think about having your students do when engaging with texts in your social studies classroom:"

- Cite specific evidence to support analysis.
- Pay attention to sourcing and what it means for context.
- Identify the argument that the author is trying to make.
- Corroborate information with other sources to distinguish between fact/opinion and reasoned judgement of the author.
- Integrate multiple viewpoints and diverse sources to develop understanding of an event/topic and make sure to note discrepancies.
- Analyze a series of events for connections.
- Look for overarching principles/concepts that is the basis for the point the author is trying to make.
- Interpret meaning of key words/phrases.
- Be sure to pay attention to images, graphics, maps, data, charts, and graphs that are connected to any text that is read.

As we break down each part of the four-step planning process, you will walk away with strategies to help you teach your students these important skills. Indeed, these strategies clearly demonstrate how reading about a historical event during an ELA block is not the same as teaching students to use these disciplinary skills to think like historians, geographers, and economists. That is why it is important for teachers to have designated instructional time specifically for social studies. According to the Council of Chief State School Officers (CCSSO, 2018), schools should "dedicate at least 45 minutes of daily instructional time to social studies in grades K–5" (p. 1). But for many elementary teachers, district instructional time allotment guidelines prevent teachers from having a social studies block, as there are just not enough minutes in the day, or they are expected to integrate other content areas with social studies. Because of this reality, you'll find Integration Idea feature boxes throughout the book that offer suggestions on how to take critical social studies concepts and disciplinary skills and embed them in other content areas.

What's in This Book

This book walks you through each part of the four-step planning process. It features more than thirty research-based activities and strategies to ensure your elementary social studies units include all the essential components. Each of the first four chapters focuses on a single step of the process.

Chapter 1, "Step 1: Making Meaning of Social Studies Standards," will help you get to know your standards by unpacking them. Then, you will use a practice specific to social studies: identifying enduring understandings within your standards. Finally, you will use these enduring understandings to craft compelling questions. A compelling question provides a hook at the beginning of the unit, guides the lessons within the unit as students look for evidence to answer the compelling question, and marks the unit's end as students answer the compelling question.

Chapter 2, "Step 2: Creating Assessments," will explain the two types of assessments, as well as how to use classroom-based assessments that focus on the claim-evidence-reasoning framework specific to social studies. You will also learn how to take assessment to the next level by planning for informed action.

Chapter 3, "Step 3: Choosing and Analyzing Primary Sources," will define what primary sources are, explain why using primary sources is important, provide resources for finding grade-appropriate primary sources, and discuss strategies for using primary sources with students as they analyze and make sense of these historical sources. Primary source analysis strategies include historical thinking, analysis charts, visual analyses, questioning, annotating, and reading portraits.

Chapter 4, "Step 4: Choosing and Analyzing Secondary Sources," will define what secondary sources are; explain why using them is important; provide resources for finding grade-appropriate secondary sources; and discuss strategies for using, analyzing, and making sense of those sources. Secondary source analysis strategies include before-reading, during-reading, and after-reading strategies.

Each of the first four chapters includes a section called Building Your Own Unit, in which you'll find two completed sample planning templates for the given step of the process, both building on respective Veterans Day units in K–2 and 3–5 grade bands. It is in this section, too, that you will have the opportunity to begin creating your own social studies unit using the planning template.

Chapter 5, "Turning Your Unit Into Daily Lesson Plans," provides a completed sample planning template for each elementary grade band (K–2 and 3–5) that can be used as is or as a guide for creating your own units. This chapter will also provide guidance for how to turn your completed planning template into daily lesson plans.

The appendices at the end of the book provide tools and templates to support your planning work. As an elementary teacher myself, I designed this process for other elementary teachers with the hope that it helps educators see the importance of social studies instruction, even at the elementary level, and how easy it can be to plan these units. Each component of the process contributes to educators' goals of improved social studies and literacy outcomes (Catts, 2021–2022; CCSSO, 2018; Haass, 2023; Minero, 2015; Pondiscio, 2023; Schwartz, 2023). But equally important, students need these skills and practices as they enter a world that demands their civic participation. For these reasons—even though all the examples used in the book are for elementary classrooms—middle and high school social studies teachers, curriculum specialists, instructional coaches, and administrators will also find the planning process and strategies beneficial.

While the book is intended to be read from start to finish, you can also go directly to chapters to find strategies and tips as you plan lessons. For example, are you planning an assessment? Check out chapter 2 (page 29). Are you looking for strategies to analyze primary sources? Check out chapter 3 (page 47). By using the easy four-step planning process outlined in this book, you can have the results of the teacher from classroom B! Your students will learn social studies content and skills *and* be prepared for civic engagement. It is my hope that this easy planning process will remind you of the importance of social studies in the elementary classroom and reignite your passion for teaching it.

CHAPTER 1

Step 1: Making Meaning of Social Studies Standards

Imagine for a moment that you are a first-year elementary teacher excited to begin the school year in your first classroom. You are equally excited to plan your first social studies lessons. You decide to start by looking through your standards document—and you are thoroughly unprepared for the number of standards you see! What do they mean, and how will you ever cover it all in one year?

Standards represent outcomes—what we want students to know and be able to do. Authors and consultants Kim Bailey and Chris Jakicic (2023) define *standards* as "the knowledge and skills states and provinces identify for student learning" (p. 29). The knowledge and skills within the standards will guide your decisions as you plan your social studies units. Therefore, identifying and making meaning of the standard or standards for your unit is the first step in the four-step planning process. Whether you are a first-year or a veteran teacher, the number of standards you are required to know and teach can be overwhelming.

This chapter's goal is to help you feel comfortable with your standards as you develop social studies units. First, we will choose and unpack your unit standards. Next, we will look at a standards practice specific to working with social studies: uncovering the enduring understandings within your standards. Identifying big ideas will aid you in writing compelling questions—the heart of social studies units, as students will grapple with them from the beginning to the end. At the end of the chapter, you will find examples of step 1 of the four-step planning process for grades K–2 and grades 3–5, and then begin creating your own unit by adding a standard, enduring understanding, and compelling question to a four-step planning process template.

Unpacking Social Studies Standards

Each state, province, or territory has its own standards document for each grade and content area. Before starting step 1 of the four-step planning process, there is a little bit of prep work you will want to do with your standards document. First, it is important to carefully read your standards document to ensure clarity about the expected student outcomes contained within the standards. Next, you will want to map your standards into instructional units by creating a list of your units and the standards you will cover in each, ensuring that all the standards are placed within a unit at some point during the year. If your state has many standards, you may have several standards per unit. However, you may have only one per unit if your state has a small number of standards. For this book, we will plan our example unit around one standard.

Now you are ready to begin step 1 of the four-step planning process: Making Meaning of Social Studies Standards. The first action is to look more closely at the outcomes contained within the standard you have chosen for the unit you are planning. These outcomes include the *knowledge* about social studies content and the *skills* students will need to understand the concepts within the content. For example, if a standard asks students to use evidence to support claims in a primary source, students must know what a primary source is (knowledge) and be able to use evidence to support claims within the source (skill). This way of decomposing standards is sometimes referred to as *unpacking* or *unwrapping* standards. Professional education consultant and author Larry Ainsworth (2015b) explains that "'unwrapping' is a simple method that all teachers in all grade levels can use to deconstruct the wording of any standard in order to know its meaning inside and out." He further explains that this process is important so that teachers can accurately teach standards and communicate to their students specific learning intentions for each unit (Ainsworth, 2015b). John Hattie, an educational researcher whose work focuses on what works best for learning in schools, finds that teacher clarity has an effect size of 0.75 (Visible Learning, n.d.). This means teachers knowing their lesson's goals and clearly communicating those goals to students can result in almost two years' worth of growth in one year's time.

So, how do you unpack your standards? Ainsworth (2015b) suggests a simple approach: underlining "teachable concepts (important nouns and noun phrases)" and setting in all capitals "the skills (verbs) that students are to demonstrate." These items represent what students should *know* and be able to *do* by the end of the unit. Figure 1.1 provides examples of unwrapped standards from kindergarten and grades 2 and 4.

Grade Level and Social Studies Discipline	Unwrapped Standard
Kindergarten Civics	IDENTIFY and EXPLAIN <u>reasons for rules</u> at home and in school.
Second-Grade Geography	CONSTRUCT <u>maps</u> of the local community that contain <u>symbols</u>, <u>labels</u>, and <u>legends</u> denoting <u>human and physical characteristics</u> of place.
Fourth-Grade Economics	DESCRIBE characteristics of a <u>market economy</u>.

Source for standard: Michigan Department of Education, n.d.

Figure 1.1: Examples of unwrapped standards.

Note that most elementary social studies standards documents focus on the four social studies disciplines of the C3 Framework: (1) civics, (2) economics, (3) geography, and (4) history. Within each of those four disciplines is specific content knowledge that students should learn and skills they should be able to exhibit for each grade level. For example, the State of Arkansas identifies a standard for grades K–4 within each of the areas of civics, economics, geography, and history and then lists specific content knowledge and skill performance expectations for each grade within that standard. Table 1.1 (page 14) is a civics standard broken down into content knowledge and skill performance expectations for kindergarten through fourth grade.

Integration Idea
ELA

When getting to know your social studies standards, it is worth taking the time to compare them to your ELA standards. Many social studies and ELA standards overlap. For example, an informational standard from the Common Core State Standards reads that students should "delineate and evaluate the argument and specific claims in a text, including the validity of the reasoning as well as the relevance and sufficiency of the evidence" (National Governors Association Center for Best Practices & Council of Chief State School Officers [NGA & CCSSO], 2010). This is similar to a history standard from the C3 Framework that states students should "use evidence to develop a claim about the past" (National Council for the Social Studies [NCSS], 2013, p. 49). This shows that you can teach and practice ELA standards while using social studies texts and sources.

Table 1.1: Civics Standard With Content Knowledge and Skill Performance Expectations

C.1: Students will understand the impact of origins, structures, and functions of institutions and laws on society and citizens. This includes personal civic rights, roles, responsibilities, and processes by which laws are made and amended.

Civic and Political Institutions				
Content Knowledge and Skill Performance Expectations				
Kindergarten	**Grade 1**	**Grade 2**	**Grade 3**	**Grade 4**
C.1.K.1 Identify the purpose of classroom or school rules in establishing communities and ways of living and working together. **Teacher Note:** This standard builds toward students relating rules to values of fairness and equality.	C.1.1.1 Connect classroom rules and a student handbook as documents that establish the values of fairness and equality in a school community. **Teacher Note:** This standard builds toward students relating founding documents to values of fairness and equality.	C.1.2.1 Identify founding documents of the United States: • Declaration of Independence • U.S. Constitution • Bill of Rights	C.1.3.1 Discuss the origins of the United States' founding documents: • Declaration of Independence • U.S. Constitution • Bill of Rights	C.1.4.1 Explain the rights and responsibilities citizens have according to the Declaration of Independence, U.S. Constitution, and Bill of Rights: • Freedoms (religion, speech, press, peaceable assembly) • Rights (personal protection, fair trial by jury, vote, fair and equal treatment under the law) • Responsibility to respect the rights and property of others

Source for standard: Arkansas Department of Education, 2022.

Spend some time looking over your state's or district's social studies standards for your grade level. Make sure that you can determine the specific content knowledge—what students need to learn and understand—within each standard and social studies discipline, as well as the specific skills or processes students will use to understand these concepts. If your standards document doesn't already list each standard's content knowledge and skill performance expectations, it is helpful to rewrite the standard with this information, similar to the structure of the third-grade history standard in figure 1.2. Knowing the content knowledge and skills for each standard is also important for future steps.

Third-Grade Standard A.3: "Identify some of the communities in Canada around the beginning of the 19th century, and describe their relationships to the land and to each other."

Content Knowledge and Skills:

- Identify various First Nations and some Métis communities in Upper and Lower Canada from 1780 to 1850.

- Identify various settler communities in Canada during this period.

- Identify some of the main factors that helped shape the development of settlements in Canada during this period.

- Describe some of the major challenges facing communities in Canada during this period.

Source: Ontario Curriculum, 2013.

Figure 1.2: Example of content knowledge and skills—third-grade history standard.

Finding the Enduring Understandings in Your Standards

After you have identified and unpacked a standard for a unit of study, the next step is to identify an enduring understanding your students will take away from the unit. Enduring understandings are issues or big ideas that have relevance over a long period of time and add meaning to our students' conceptual understandings, signifying learning that goes beyond the memorization of dates and facts. Without a big idea, the purpose of your unit can be confusing for students as they struggle to make connections or answer the question, Why do we have to learn this? Therefore, enduring understandings provide the focus and purpose for social studies units.

Integration Idea
ELA, Mathematics, and Science

It is important to remember our discussion on disciplinary literacy from the introduction (page 1) when thinking about your social studies standards and the connections across multiple content areas. Literacy educator Timothy Shanahan (2017) describes disciplinary literacy as "apprenticing young readers into reading like disciplinary experts." This goes beyond teaching basic reading skills used to understand texts in various content areas. It means we must help students think like historians, geographers, mathematicians, and scientists when working with the various texts these experts use. Thus, we must help students "grasp the ways literacy is used to create, disseminate, and critique information in the various disciplines" (Shanahan, 2017). For example, geographers might use maps to explain how elevation influenced a region's development. Teachers can make cross-curricular connections to mathematics by measuring elevation differences between cities in that region and connections to science by looking at the human-environment interactions as that region developed. However, I cannot stress this enough: Just using social studies texts or sources like maps in various content areas is not the same as teaching social studies. We must help students use the skills and processes of experts within social studies disciplines if we want to truly teach social studies.

Some standards documents communicate enduring understandings through themes. The NCSS (n.d.b) has identified ten themes that should be found in social studies programs. While these themes are often not explicitly stated in most state and provincial standards, they are implicitly inferred within the standards' content and skills. Table 1.2 lists NCSS's ten themes and key ideas within them, as well as unit topics you might focus on within these themes.

The themes themselves can represent an enduring understanding, or you, as the teacher, can refine the key idea to get to the ultimate enduring understanding connected to your unit. For example, let's say a K–2 grade teacher chooses the following standard for an economics unit: "Explain how scarcity necessitates decision making" (NCSS, 2013, p. 36). A connected key idea from table 1.2 is that *wants often exceed the availability of resources.* This is an

Table 1.2: Ten Themes of Social Studies

Theme	Key Idea	Unit Topics
1. Culture	The beliefs, values, traditions, and way of life of a group of people can change over time.	Geography History
2. Time, Continuity, and Change	Societies, people, and nations experience continuity and change over time.	History
3. People, Places, and Environments	The relationship between people and their physical world undergoes change over time.	Geography Regional Studies World Cultures
4. Individual Development and Identity	Identity is shaped by an individual's culture and lived experiences.	Family Communities
5. Individuals, Groups, and Institutions	Political, economic, and social organizations enable us to manage our daily lives.	Government History
6. Power, Authority, and Governance	The structures of power, authority, and government have developed over time.	Government Civics History
7. Production, Distribution, and Consumption	Wants often exceed the availability of resources.	Economics
8. Science, Technology, and Society	Social and cultural changes are often affected by changes in science and technology.	History Geography Economics Civics Government
9. Global Connections	Global connections affect decisions made at the local, national, and international levels.	Geography Culture Economics History Government Technology
10. Civic Ideals and Practices	Understanding civic ideals and practices is critical to citizenship.	Civics History

Source: NCSS, n.d.b.

enduring understanding that might work for a second-grade student. The teacher could also simplify it for kindergarten students as *we don't always get everything we want.* This table represents themes suggested by one organization— it is by no means an exhaustive list.

The Missouri State Department of Elementary and Secondary Education; CCSSO; and ACT, Inc. (2001) identify themes within the four disciplines of social studies: (1) civics, (2) economics, (3) geography, and (4) history. Many of these themes are similar to those in table 1.2 (page 17) created by NCSS, but more succinct. These themes are described in table 1.3.

Table 1.3: Themes in U.S. Civics, Economics, Geography, and History

Civics	Economics	Geography	History
Civic life, politics, and governance systems	Limited resources and choice	Places, regions, locations	Change and continuity in political systems
Principles and ideals of U.S. democracy	How markets work	Physical systems (spatial perspective)	Interactions of people, cultures, and ideas
Purpose, structure, and functions of the U.S. government	Economic systems	Human systems (spatial perspective)	Economic and technological changes
Roles, rights, privileges, and responsibilities of U.S. citizens	Economic interdependence	Environment and society (spatial perspective)	Comparative history of major developments
Relationships among governments and people that cross national boundaries			

Source: Missouri Department of Elementary and Secondary Education; CCSSO; & ACT, Inc., 2001, p. 12.

Let's use one of the kindergarten civics standards that we unpacked earlier in the chapter to practice finding enduring understandings within standards (see figure 1.1, page 13): "Identify and explain reasons for rules at home and in school" (Michigan Department of Education, n.d.). Look again at table 1.2 (page 17).

Which themes deal with *reasons for rules*, which was identified as the content we want students to learn when unpacking this standard? You might have chosen the following themes: culture; individual development and identity; individuals, groups, and institutions; power, authority, and governance; and civic ideals and practices.

Now look at table 1.3. Which themes deal with reasons for rules in this list? You might have chosen several from the Civics column: civic life, politics, and governance systems; principles and ideals of U.S. democracy; and roles, rights, privileges, and responsibilities of U.S. citizens. Next, think about what connects each of these themes. In this example, we want students to understand reasons for rules. Why? Rules create order and structure in our lives. Rules are similar to laws, and students need to understand that obeying laws is one of our civic duties as citizens. This is the enduring understanding we want students to walk away with at the end of the unit. Now that you've identified the enduring understanding, it's time to write a compelling question.

Integration Idea
ELA

Many enduring understandings in social studies are also big ideas in fiction texts used in ELA. When reading texts with your class in ELA that connect to big ideas you're also studying in social studies, be explicit in helping students see those connections. For example, if you are reading a book and the main character's problem is getting in trouble for not following the rules, you could make a connection to the enduring understanding that you are also learning about in social studies—for example, we need to follow rules because they create order and structure in our lives and communities.

Writing Compelling Questions

Compelling questions play a critical role in each part of your unit. They provide a hook at the beginning of the unit, guide the lessons within the unit as students look for evidence to answer the compelling question, and mark the unit's end as students answer the compelling question. You may be more familiar with centering lessons around an *essential* question as opposed to a *compelling* question. Let's take a closer look at the similarities and differences between these two terms before we use the enduring understanding we identified to write a compelling question.

Educators Jay McTighe and Grant Wiggins (2013) introduce the criteria and purpose of essential questions in their book *Essential Questions: Opening Doors to Student Understanding.* According to McTighe and Wiggins (2013), the goal of essential questions is to "make our unit plans more likely to yield focused and thoughtful learning and learners" (p. 17). McTighe and Wiggins (2013) go on to explain that essential questions also:

- Signal that inquiry is a key goal of education.
- Make it more likely that the unit will be intellectually engaging.
- Help to clarify and prioritize standards for teachers.
- Provide transparency for students.
- Encourage and model metacognition for students.
- Provide opportunities for intra- and interdisciplinary connections.
- Support meaningful differentiation. (p. 17)

Now that you understand the purposes of essential questions, let's define what makes an essential question. Wiggins (2015) states that *essential questions* meet the following criteria:

- They stimulate ongoing thinking and inquiry.
- They're arguable, with multiple plausible answers.
- They raise further questions.
- They spark discussion and debate.
- They demand evidence and reasoning because varying answers exist.
- They point to big ideas and pressing issues.
- They fruitfully recur throughout the unit or year.
- The answers proposed are tentative and may change in light of new experiences and deepening understanding.

Compelling questions, on the other hand, appear in the NCSS's (2013) *The College, Career, and Civic Life (C3) Framework for Social Studies State Standards* and reflect a nuance specific to this content area. But first, it's important to note that the purpose of compelling questions within the Inquiry Design Model—put forth by the writers of the C3 Framework—is similar to that of essential questions, with a focus on achieving both rigor and relevance

(Swan et al., 2018). In other words, compelling questions need to "represent big content ideas and they need to express those ideas in ways that resonate with those things that students know and value" (Swan et al., 2018, p. 31). This is true for students of every age.

First, compelling questions must be open ended, meaning they have no single right or wrong answer. Compelling questions must not only be open ended but also, S. G. Grant (2013) adds, have two additional criteria—that is, they must be (1) meaty, or "reflect an enduring issue, concern, or debate in social studies and it has to draw on multiple disciplines" (which satisfies the purpose of representing big content ideas by covering multiple content topics), and (2) student friendly (which satisfies the purpose of focusing on those things that students know and value). Therefore, a small but important distinction between essential questions and compelling questions is that the latter create relevance by addressing "problems and issues found in and across the academic disciplines that make up social studies" (Grant, 2013). Details about real people, places, and situations make questions compelling to students, as do connections to their own lived experiences (home, school, and friends) and their communities.

When crafting your own compelling questions, think about the following three items.

1. What are the big ideas or enduring understandings that your standard is trying to get students to think about?

2. Which type of compelling question best matches the big ideas?

3. Does what you wrote meet the criteria for a strong compelling question (is it open ended, meaty, and student friendly)?

The first question—What are the big ideas or enduring understandings that your standard is trying to get students to think about?—was the work that you did in the previous section, Finding the Enduring Understandings in Your Standards. You will use that big idea as you look at the next question.

Question number two asks, "Which type of compelling question best matches the big ideas?" There are many different types of compelling questions. The type of compelling question you write will depend on the focus of your chosen standards for the unit, as well as the big idea you want your students to think about as they learn the content. Table 1.4 (page 22) describes and provides examples for ten types of compelling questions from Swan and colleagues' (2018) book *Inquiry Design Model: Building Inquiries in Social Studies*.

Table 1.4: Types and Examples of Compelling Questions

Type of Compelling Question	Definition	Example
Broad Brush	"Broad brush questions offer teachers and students opportunities to think and act on a large scale." (p. 35)	"What is justice?" (p. 35)
Case Study	Case-study questions "help teachers and students look deeply into an idea, action, or social condition, and then judge that phenomena against one or more bigger constructs." (p. 35)	"Did the printing press preserve the past or invent the future?" (p. 36)
Personalized	Personalized questions give "students the occasion to see themselves directly reflected in an inquiry." (p. 36)	"Why do I have to be responsible?" (p. 37)
Analytic	Analytic questions "examine the component dimensions of an idea, event, or phenomenon . . . to see the causes, influences, implications, and outcomes that revolve around it." (p. 37)	"Did industrialization make life better for everyone?" (p. 37)
Comparative	Comparative questions help teachers and students "analyze and compare components of multiple phenomena." (p. 41)	"Which is better, a map or a globe?" (p. 38)
Evaluative	Evaluative questions "call for students to make a judgment on the issue under study." (p. 38)	"Was the American Revolution avoidable?" (p. 38)
Problem Based	Problem-based questions offer students an opportunity to "propose potential solutions to a social problem." (p. 41)	"Should freedom be sacrificed in the name of national security?" (p. 39)
Word Play	Word-play questions "juxtapose different meanings of words and ideas." (p. 41)	"Is free trade worth the price?" (p. 40)
Ironic	Ironic questions "consider meanings below the surface of an idea." (p. 40)	"Is greed good?" (p. 40)
Mystery	Mystery questions "ask students to pursue a mystery" and "track the elements of an unanswered question." (pp. 40–41)	"What's the real story behind the Starving Years?" (p. 40)

Source for quotes: Swan et al., 2018.

Question number three asks, "Does what you wrote meet the criteria for a strong compelling question?" In other words, evaluate the compelling question to determine whether it truly is compelling.

Let's practice evaluating compelling questions. Use the following three questions to determine whether the compelling question, Is compromise always fair?—from a fifth-grade inquiry about the Constitutional Convention—is a good one.

1. **Is it open ended?** Is there more than one plausible answer? At first, this feels like a closed-ended question because students will answer either yes or no. But actually, this is considered an open-ended, compelling question because there is no single correct answer; there is evidence from the sources to support a yes or no answer. Students might say, "Yes, compromise is always fair," or they might say, "No, compromise is not always fair." And in both cases, they would be able to find evidence to support their thinking.

2. **Is it meaty?** Does it represent big or multiple content ideas? Yes, because students will need to provide evidence from the Virginia Plan, the New Jersey Plan, and the Connecticut Plan to support whether the compromises made at the Constitutional Convention were fair.

3. **Is it student friendly?** Do students know and care about the big idea within the question? Yes, because all students want things to be fair. Asking students whether fairness is always achieved through compromise will grab their attention, and more than likely, they can all share an example of a time when they felt they weren't treated fairly.

Table 1.5 (page 24) contains examples of compelling questions for grades K–5. As you read each one, think about how it meets the criteria of a compelling question. For example, the third-grade question, Does it matter how leaders are chosen?, is open ended because students could provide evidence to support an answer of yes or no; it is meaty because students will need to learn about the process of choosing leaders in their community, state, and country; and it is student friendly because students participate in choosing leaders in their school, whether it is for student council representatives or choosing the captain of the football team at recess.

Table 1.5: Examples of Compelling Questions for Grades K–5

Grade	Topic	Possible Compelling Question
Kindergarten	Civics and Government	Are all rules good rules?
First	Economics	What choices do we make with our money?
Second	Geography	How do we shape our environment?
Third	Civics and Government	Does it matter how leaders are chosen?
Fourth	Geography	Did the American Dream come true for immigrants who came to New York?
Fifth	History	Why do countries declare independence?

Source: Adapted from Grant, 2013.

Let's return to the kindergarten civics standard we were using earlier and practice crafting our own compelling question. The standard was: "Identify and explain reasons for rules at home and in school" (Michigan Department of Education, n.d.).

1. **What are the big ideas or enduring understandings that your standard is trying to get students to think about?** In this example, we decided that we wanted students to understand reasons for rules—that rules create order and structure in our lives and that obeying rules (and laws) is one of our civic duties as citizens.

2. **Which type of compelling question best matches the big ideas?** Based on our enduring understanding, we want students to make personal connections to this standard—to understand how it applies to their everyday lives. The best match would be a personalized compelling question. There is an example compelling question related to rules for a kindergarten standard in table 1.5. It states, *Are all rules good rules?* However, I'm not sure that really encompasses our enduring understanding; we want students to understand *why* we have rules. What if we used this for a compelling question: *Why do we have rules?*

3. **Does your compelling question meet the criteria for a strong one (that is, open ended, meaty, and student friendly)?** This question is open ended, as there are multiple reasons why we have rules. It is

meaty in that students will learn about rules at school, home, and in their community, and it is student friendly because all students have rules imposed on them by others.

Thinking through these three reflective questions has ensured that we have a strong compelling question—Why do we have rules?—for our kindergarten unit on reasons for rules.

Sometimes you don't have to start from scratch when writing compelling questions—you can revise questions from within curricular materials. For example, what if you already have a curriculum that provides an essential question for each unit? Take time to study the essential question and decide whether it really is essential and whether it is compelling. Sometimes questions don't meet the essential question criteria because there is only one correct answer. For example, What is a citizen? The definition of a citizen is the one answer needed to answer this question.

Sometimes questions meet the criteria of an essential question but don't require the rigor and relevance needed to be considered a compelling question. For example, What does it mean to be a citizen? This is a good essential question, but it isn't really compelling. It is meaty in the sense that students will need to learn a lot of content about the rights and responsibilities of being a citizen, but it isn't student friendly in terms of creating relevance for elementary students. If it does not satisfy the criteria of a compelling question, think about how you can revise it using the three preceding prompts for crafting your own. For example, What does it mean to be a citizen? could become this: Can one person's voice make a difference? Now students can relate because they will have experienced a time when their voice made a difference for a friend or sibling, but they will also have experienced a time when their voice alone didn't change their circumstance. Now you have their attention, *and* you've set them up to learn about civic duties, such as voting and serving on a jury.

Building Your Own Unit

Now that you know how to identify and unpack your standards and use them to identify an enduring understanding that guides the crafting of a compelling question, it's time to begin building your own social studies unit. Figure 1.3 (page 26) shows an example of step 1 of the four-step planning process for grades K–2.

Topic or Unit:	Veterans Day

Step 1: Making Meaning of Standards

Standard: D2.His.3.K-2. GENERATE questions about <u>individuals and groups</u> who have shaped a <u>significant historical change</u>.

Enduring Understanding: Soldiers make sacrifices because they want to protect their country and its citizens.

Compelling Question: What is a hero?

Source for standard: NCSS, 2013.

Figure 1.3: Step 1 of the four-step planning process example for grades K–2.

Figure 1.4 shows an example of step 1 of the four-step planning process for grades 3–5.

Topic or Unit:	Veterans Day

Step 1: Making Meaning of Standards

Standard: D2.His.6.3-5. DESCRIBE how people's <u>perspectives</u> shaped the <u>historical sources</u> they created.

Enduring Understanding: Our beliefs and values affect our actions.

Compelling Question: How do people's perspectives influence their decisions?

Source for standard: NCSS, 2013.

Figure 1.4: Step 1 of the four-step planning process example for grades 3–5.

Use the reproducible "The Four-Step Planning Process Template" (page 128) in appendix A to begin building your own social studies unit. At this point, complete only step 1—identifying a standard from your standards document, making meaning of the standard using the steps in this chapter, identifying an enduring understanding, and writing a compelling question using the questions in this chapter as a guide.

Summary

The goal of this book is to provide a four-step process for planning social studies units. In this chapter, you learned how to complete step 1 of the unit planning process: Making Meaning of Social Studies Standards. This step included a sequence for using standards for your unit: (1) choose a standard for a unit focus, (2) make meaning of the standard, (3) identify an enduring understanding within that standard, and (4) use that big idea to craft a compelling question. This chapter also explained the difference between an essential question and a compelling question and the importance of making sure that questions in social studies are truly compelling. Then you learned how to use the enduring understanding to write a compelling question. The compelling question is important because it is used throughout your unit—it hooks students at the beginning because it creates rigor and relevance, it guides the lesson as students use sources to find evidence to answer the question, and it will eventually provide the foundation for assessment at the end of a unit. Creating assessments is covered in the next chapter.

CHAPTER 2

Step 2: Creating Assessments

Now equipped with the ways to decode standards—choosing and unpacking your standard, identifying an enduring understanding you have chosen for your unit, and writing a compelling question—once again take on the perspective of that first-year elementary teacher. You realize that *you* understand the standard, but how will you know whether your *students* have mastered the standard? Maybe even more importantly, how will you know whether your students have internalized the enduring understanding?

This chapter will look at step 2 of the four-step planning process: Creating Assessments. We analyze the difference between formative and summative assessments and explore what each of these assessment types looks like within a social studies unit. We also look at what makes social studies assessments different from other content areas as students apply the enduring understanding to their lives as they "do" social studies. At the end of the chapter, you will find examples of step 2 of the four-step planning process for grades K–2 and grades 3–5, and then you will continue creating your own unit by adding a classroom-based assessment and a "doing" social studies activity to the four-step planning process template you started in chapter 1 (page 11).

Assessment Types

First, let's make sure that we have a common understanding of what we mean when referring to an assessment. An assessment is not just an end-of-unit procedure. According to authors Jeff Flygare, Jan K. Hoegh, and Tammy Heflebower (2022), an *assessment* should occur throughout the unit to inform teaching, learning, and instructional decisions. There are two main types of assessments: (1) *formative* and (2) *summative*. Bailey and Jakicic (2023) explain that formative assessments serve as "checkpoints to gather evidence of essential skills and concept attainment throughout the instructional journey within a unit" (p. 29). *Formative assessments* are diagnostic in nature and allow the teacher to identify students who aren't understanding the skills and content needed to master the standard. In turn, the teacher can respond with intervention or reteaching. In other words, formative assessments should inform the teaching and learning process; as professors of educational leadership Douglas Fisher and Nancy Frey (2014) explain, it can improve instructional methods and provide feedback for students. *Summative assessments*, on the other hand, evaluate student learning of content knowledge and skill proficiency at the end of a learning cycle. It measures *student competency*—the student's content knowledge or skill proficiency found in the standard being assessed—after an instructional phase is complete (Fisher & Frey, 2014). Whereas formative assessments are used to check for understanding, summative assessments are most often used to assign a grade.

You will use ongoing formative assessment throughout a social studies unit, sometimes multiple times throughout a lesson. The formative assessments you use will allow you to check students' understanding of the content you are teaching, as well as the skills to access that content. For example, in the Veterans Day unit for K–2 from chapter 1 (figure 1.3, page 26), students need to be able to define the word *veteran* and identify various ways that communities and individuals honor veterans before they can answer the compelling question, What is a hero? There are various tasks you can use to assess the aforementioned content knowledge and skills. You could ask students to define (orally or written) the term *veteran*. You could ask students to draw or write about one or two ways to honor veterans. Additional types of formative tasks to assess knowledge and skills include listing or ranking problems, reasons, challenges, or key features; annotating sources, such as maps or photographs; making a timeline; creating charts or graphic organizers, such as T-charts or Venn diagrams; and participating in a debate (Swan et al., 2018).

Students are asked to answer the compelling question at the end of a social studies unit. This serves as a summative assessment because students demonstrate comprehension of the standard by using facts and details from sources, and it provides students a chance to connect the content to the enduring understanding and other big ideas. For these reasons, it's most effective to use a nontraditional summative assessment format—classroom-based assessment—for answering the compelling question. Educators Jo Lewkowicz and Constant Leung (2021) define a *classroom-based assessment* as "any teacher-led classroom activity designed to find out about students' performance on curriculum tasks that would yield information regarding their understanding as well as their need for further support and scaffolding with reference to their situated learning needs" (p. 48). The unit you are building will end with students answering the compelling question using evidence from the sources they analyze, which will be covered in chapters 3 (page 47) and 4 (page 81). Answering the compelling question is the classroom-based assessment, and one way to design that assessment is by using the claim-evidence-reasoning framework.

Claim-Evidence-Reasoning Framework

The goal at the end of your social studies unit is for students to be able to answer the compelling question you wrote in step 1 of the four-step planning process. A strategy for answering compelling questions in a classroom-based assessment is to use the claim-evidence-reasoning (CER) framework. Using CER, students create an evidence-based argument, or claim, with reasoning that describes how the evidence supports the claim. It also provides a scaffold to support students' writing of evidence-based arguments. Table 2.1 defines each component of the CER framework as it is used in social studies classroom–based assessments.

Table 2.1: Claim-Evidence-Reasoning Framework Components

Component	Definition
Claim	The writer's argument or stance in response to the compelling question; the claim is arguable
Evidence	The information from both primary and secondary sources a writer uses to support the claim; the evidence is not arguable—it is fact
Reasoning	The explanation of how the evidence supports the claim

Next, let's look at a written classroom-based assessment example based on the sample four-step planning process template (see figure 1.3, page 26) we started in chapter 1 (page 11). The compelling question is, What is a hero?

Here is a sample classroom-based assessment response using the CER framework:

> A **hero** is someone who makes sacrifices to help others. A veteran is a hero because sometimes they lose their life protecting our freedoms. The photograph of the Vietnam Veterans Day ceremony shows people honoring veterans who had died with flowers. This shows that veterans are heroes because not everyone is willing to make this kind of sacrifice.

The first two sentences are the claim because they answer the compelling question ("A hero is someone who makes sacrifices to help others") and include a reason for that answer ("A veteran is a hero because sometimes they lose their life protecting our freedoms").

The third sentence is the evidence because it contains information from analyzed sources that supports the claim ("The photograph of the Vietnam Veterans Day ceremony shows people honoring veterans who had died with flowers").

The fourth sentence is the reasoning because it explains how the evidence supports the claim ("This shows that veterans are heroes because not everyone is willing to make this kind of sacrifice").

Keep in mind that this is the type of classroom-based assessment that a fourth or fifth grader might produce, and the CER framework looks different for lower elementary grade students. Kindergarten students might produce a claim through discussion while the teacher writes it down (or students could copy the claim onto their paper if it's later in the school year). The claim for

Integration Idea
Science and ELA

The CER framework is applicable to all content areas. Exposure to the terms *claim*, *evidence*, and *reasoning* and the process of using the framework throughout several content areas (and multiple times a day) will result in quicker student independence with this type of writing and thinking than if they use it only in social studies. In science, students make a claim, use evidence from scientific data to support their claim, and use reasoning that involves a rule or scientific principle (Brunsell, 2012). For example, students could make the claim that air is matter even though we can't see it, use evidence from an investigation with inflating balloons, then use reasoning to explain how the evidence (adding air to the balloon changes the balloon's shape even though we can't see the air) supports the claim. In ELA, students use the CER framework in writing about literature, such as in a literary essay. For example, students could make a claim about a story's theme, use quotes or events from the story as evidence, then use reasoning to explain how the evidence supports the claim.

our previous example might be, *Veterans are heroes because they make sacrifices to help people.* The teacher could then lead a discussion with students to find evidence supporting their thinking. For example, they could discuss what details from the sources they analyzed show examples of how soldiers help people.

The teacher may need to provide the reasoning using a think-aloud for students at this age. For example, the teacher might say, "In this photograph, soldiers are helping a wounded soldier that was hurt during a war. They are helping us by keeping our country safe. Since soldiers help us stay safe, they are heroes." Then, students might provide their evidence by drawing a picture of a soldier and labeling it with the single word *hero*. Depending on your students' prior knowledge and experience using evidence and reasoning to support claims, you can use a gradual release of responsibility model to build students' skills. You can write claims with evidence and reasoning as a whole class and then slowly release parts of the CER framework to students throughout the school year as they gain the skills to work independently. See figure 2.1 (page 34) for a suggested progression.

Strategies to Build CER Skills

The following sections detail several strategies that you can use to build your students' CER skills.

Line Arrangement

This first strategy is a combination of value lineups and fold the line activities. This strategy will help students practice using evidence and reasoning to make claims with topics they are already familiar with. To use the strategy, have students evaluate a statement, and then line up according to their degree of agreement or disagreement. After forming a single line, fold the line in half so that the students who most strongly agreed and disagreed with one another are now face-to-face. Students then discuss their evidence and reasoning to support their claim, or position, on the statement. Students strengthen their claim through argumentation and develop listening skills as they consider others' perspectives. This strategy can be used with students of all grade levels to practice using evidence and reasoning to make claims. For example, lower elementary grade students begin to learn about making claims by thinking about statements like *dogs are better than cats.* Upper elementary grade students can develop their skills in supporting claims by providing historical evidence and reasoning as they discuss statements like *rules should always be followed.*

Claim-Evidence-Reasoning Progression	Example
Whole-class discussion leads to a claim statement, the teacher writes down the claim, and students draw an example of their evidence.	Veterans are heroes because they make sacrifices to help people. (Students draw a picture of a soldier.)
Whole-class discussion leads to a claim statement; the students write down the claim and write about their evidence.	Veterans are heroes. They fight in wars to protect their country.
Students independently write a claim statement and explain evidence, including the source.	Veterans are heroes because they make sacrifices to help people. The book *Veterans: Heroes in Our Neighborhood* shows veterans who were once soldiers on naval ships (Pfundstein, 2012). They were far away from home, which means they were making a sacrifice to protect their country.
Students independently write a claim statement, explain evidence with a source, and orally explain how their evidence connects to the claim.	Veterans are heroes because they make sacrifices to help people. The book *Veterans: Heroes in Our Neighborhood* shows veterans who were once soldiers on naval ships. (The student would then explain to the teacher that soldiers leave their homes and families to protect their country, which makes them heroes.)
Students independently write a claim statement, explain evidence with a source, and explain how their evidence connects to the claim.	Veterans are heroes because they make sacrifices to help people. The book *Veterans: Heroes in Our Neighborhood* shows veterans who were once soldiers on naval ships. This shows that soldiers leave their homes and families to protect their country, which takes a lot of courage and is a characteristic of a hero.

Figure 2.1: Sample claim-evidence-reasoning progression.

Every-Pupil Response

Every-pupil response uses response cards (holding up a card that reads either yes or no), hand signals (indicating with a thumbs-up or thumbs-down), or movement (standing or sitting). This strategy ensures that all students participate, and the teacher can quickly assess students' position on or understanding of a topic. It is useful when initially teaching students claims and evidence writing or as a quick formative assessment after they have had experience using evidence to support claims.

Integration Idea
ELA

To provide additional practice for using evidence and reasoning to make claims, use the line arrangement before reading stories in ELA that contain characters with internal struggles. For example, in the novel *Shiloh* (Naylor, 2000), the main character wrestles with whether it is OK to keep the secret from his parents that he is hiding a dog from an abusive owner. You could have students participate in the line arrangement activity prior to reading the book by asking students about their level of agreement with this claim: *Children should never keep secrets from their parents.* After reading the book, you could return to the same claim and have students complete the activity again but with evidence from the text.

To use the every-pupil response to determine which students understand how to match evidence to claims, first state a claim and read pieces of evidence from sources. Give students a moment to decide whether the evidence supports the claim, and then respond using whatever technique you have chosen for them. For example, when stating the claim, *the president is not the most important person in the government,* teachers could read evidence statements and then have students stand up if they agree that the evidence supports the claim or sit down if the evidence does not support the claim. The following is an example of an evidence statement: *the system of checks and balances gives equal power to each branch.* This evidence supports the claim because it explains that there are many important people in government. However, the statement, *the Constitution describes three branches of government,* would not support the claim because, although it is true, it does not connect to who is most important in government.

Claim-Evidence Connection

A third strategy is to provide students opportunities to practice finding evidence in texts that support claims before writing their own claim and evidence statements. For example, in the book *The Monarchs Are Missing: A Butterfly Mystery* by Rebecca E. Hirsch (2018), the author makes the claim that monarchs are disappearing and need to be protected. You could provide students with this claim statement before reading the book and then tell them to listen for evidence to support the author's claim as you read the text aloud. Literacy coaches Daniel M. Argentar, Katherine A. N. Gillies, Maureen M. Rubenstein, and Brian R. Wise (2021) write that as students gain independence with finding evidence to support claims, you can add the challenge of having them find evidence that refutes the claim.

Another variation of this strategy is using a claim-evidence T-chart. After introducing the compelling question at the beginning of the unit, you could introduce several claims. These claims would be written on the left-hand side of a T-chart. After analyzing each primary or secondary source, work with your students to write evidence from each source on the right-hand side of the T-chart that supports each claim on the left-hand side. If you are working with students who are new to claims and evidence, you could provide evidence statements from the sources, and students would decide which claim they support. For example, you might provide the following claims for the compelling question, What is a hero?

- A hero is someone who sacrifices to help others.
- A hero is someone who fights for freedom.
- A hero is someone who puts others before themselves.

Then, you might lead your students through analyzing a photograph of visitors at the Vietnam Veterans Memorial wall in Washington, DC. Students might decide this photograph supports the idea that sometimes a soldier's sacrifice includes losing their life to help protect their country. On the T-chart across from the claim, *a hero is someone who sacrifices to help others,* the class could record the following as evidence: *The Vietnam Veterans Memorial wall is a way to remember soldiers who have lost their lives protecting their country.*

Figure 2.2 shows an example of what this T-chart might look like as the class is working on it.

Color-Coding

This strategy is helpful when students start writing their own CER statements. This type of writing is difficult, so students often need guidance when using the CER framework to ensure they have all the required components. Color-coding provides a clear visual so students can identify required components in a mentor paragraph and ensure they've included all the components

Compelling Question: What is a hero?	
Claims	**Evidence**
A hero is someone who sacrifices to help others.	The Vietnam Veterans Memorial wall is a way to remember soldiers who have lost their lives protecting their country. (Or: The photograph of the Vietnam Veterans Day Ceremony shows people honoring veterans who had died with flowers.)
A hero is someone who fights for freedom.	
A hero is someone who puts others before themselves.	

Figure 2.2: Sample T-chart of claims and evidence.

in their own writing. Assign a color for each of the required writing parts. For example, claims are red, evidence is yellow, and reasoning is blue. Then, provide sample paragraphs of claim-evidence-reasoning and have students use highlighters or colored pencils to color-code each component. After students have had sufficient practice color-coding sample paragraphs, have them color-code the claims, evidence, and reasoning in their own CERs to ensure they've included each required component. For example:

> **Veterans are heroes.** *This is a claim, so students should color-code it in red.*
>
> **The book *Veterans: Heroes in Our Neighborhood* (Pfundstein, 2012) shows veterans who were once soldiers on naval ships.** *This is evidence, so students should color-code it in yellow.*
>
> **This shows that soldiers leave their home and family to protect their country, which takes a lot of courage and is a characteristic of a hero.** *This is reasoning, so students should color-code it in blue.*

Integration Idea
ELA

Identify claims that you can pull from the texts used in your ELA block. You can use this opportunity to build your students' claims, evidence, and reasoning skills. For example, in a text from TextProject (textproject.org), students are learning about the reasons why some countries are phasing out small coins. You could introduce the text by having students make a claim about pennies. Their claim might be *The United States should continue using pennies* or *The United States should not continue using pennies*. Before reading the article, they can provide evidence based on their own knowledge and experience with pennies. After the article, they can revise their support of the claim with evidence from the text.

Rubrics

A final strategy is using rubrics to ensure your students know the success criteria for writing claims using the CER framework. Providing students with rubrics helps them understand the criteria for success and provides a way for students to assess their own writing, clearly understand teacher feedback, and set goals for themselves. Figure 2.3 is an elementary rubric for a social studies classroom-based assessment.

The goal is for students to be at the proficient level. For students needing enrichment or extension, teachers can use the criteria at the exemplary level to challenge them to go deeper with their ability to write and support claims.

When you first introduce the rubric to your students, you can pair it with a mentor classroom-based assessment, like the example on page 31. Lead your students in a discussion about how they would score the classroom-based assessment using the rubric. You could follow up with a discussion regarding the feedback they might give the student who wrote this classroom-based assessment—what did they do well and what could be their next steps?

If you choose to teach one step of the CER framework at a time, you can reveal just one line of the rubric at a time so that students can see what proficiency looks like and use it to assess mentor texts as previously discussed.

	1 Beginning	2 Developing	3 Proficient	4 Exemplary	Score
Claim	The claim is absent or unclear.	The claim is unclear, inaccurate, or vague, or the reason stated does not provide support for the claim.	The claim is clear and accurate and includes at least one reason to support the claim.	The claim is clear and accurate and includes at least two reasons to support the claim.	Claim Score:
Evidence	The evidence is absent or unclear.	The evidence included is vague or inaccurate, or the source is not included.	The evidence is from at least one source that supports the claim, and the source is included.	The evidence is from at least two sources that support the claim, and the source is included.	Evidence Score:
Reasoning	The reasoning is absent or unclear.	The reasoning tries to connect one piece of evidence to the claim, but the connection isn't clear or is confusing.	The reasoning clearly connects at least one piece of evidence from a primary or secondary source to support the claim.	The reasoning clearly connects at least two pieces of evidence from primary or secondary sources to support the claim.	Reasoning Score:

Source: Adapted from Kansas State Department of Education, 2023.

Figure 2.3: Elementary classroom-based assessment rubric.

Classroom-Based Assessment Student Product Options

So far, we have looked at classroom-based assessments that result in a written product. But not all of these assessments must end with this type of final product. There are many other ways for students to answer the compelling question using the CER framework. Table 2.2 has classroom-based assessment product suggestions with the grade bands they would be appropriate for.

Table 2.2: Classroom-Based Assessment Product Suggestions

Product	Explanation	Grade Band
Drawing	Students draw a picture (with or without labels or captions) to represent their claim.	K–2
Living Museum	Students work together to create a scene that demonstrates their claim. When the teacher comes around and pushes the imaginary button, the scene comes to life. The teacher can require older students to demonstrate evidence and reasoning through the oral part of the presentation.	K–5
Storyboard	Students create a storyboard to represent their claim in pictures, labeling their claim and evidence with sources. During a presentation, students explain how their storyboard supports their claim, identify their evidence and sources within the storyboard, and explain how their evidence supports the claim (reasoning). The number of boxes in the storyboard can vary by grade, as well as whether students write or orally explain each box. This product works best with historical events.	2–5
Letter	Students write a letter to a friend or family member using their claim, evidence, and reasoning as the content of their letter.	3–5
Song or Poem	Students write a song or poem that answers the compelling question.	3–5
Infographics	An infographic is a visual representation of information using text, images, and data. Students create (or the teacher can provide a template for) an infographic that answers the compelling question using the CER framework. The images could represent the evidence while the matching text could be the reasoning.	3–5
News Show or Podcast	Students create a news show or podcast where the interview questions and responses will answer the compelling question using the CER framework. Students work together to write the script ensuring all components of the rubric are included and then present their news report to the class.	3–5

Doing Social Studies: Civic Action

Summing up the research of authors Scott McLeod and Dean Shareski (2018), as well as Jal Mehta and Sarah Fine (2019), Driscoll and McCusker (2022) explain that "deeper learning is more common in learning environments characterized by authenticity and real-world learning" (p. 36). In other words, it's about students not just learning but *developing* content knowledge and skills they can take into the real world later. Therefore, while teaching about citizenship is important, we must also provide students with experiences that mirror those of actual citizens. Most students never actively participate as citizens before leaving high school (Driscoll & McCusker, 2022), yet we expect these same students to be productive citizens.

Lisa Guilfoile and Brady Delander (2014) of the Education Commission of the States confirm that students who receive high-quality civic education are more likely to vote, discuss politics, contact the government, and take part in civic activities like volunteering. This shows that students need to be civically active, even at a young age. According to Driscoll and McCusker (2022), "We can't develop active citizens if civic education does not include performing real acts of citizenship" (p. 4). Therefore, students must not wait until the future to be active citizens; they can be active citizens today. As Guilfoile and Delander (2014) state, "Students cannot be expected to be civically engaged simply by reading. They can only learn how to be civically engaged by *being* civically engaged" (p. 4). Students need to participate in the same kinds of activities that they will participate in as adults. According to Meira Levinson and Peter Levine (2013), educators and civics writers for the C3 Framework, just as we improve reading fluency by reading and develop automaticity with adding by practicing addition, "students need similar guided experiential opportunities to take informed action throughout their K–12 schooling in order to learn how to engage productively in civic life" (p. 339).

There are two types of civic practices that students can participate in to "do" social studies, one of which Levinson and Levine (2013) capture in the preceding quote: taking informed action. According to Swan and colleagues (2018), these types of activities provide opportunities for students "to see how . . . ideas play out in the real world" (p. 129). Students demonstrate their understanding of the content knowledge and skills while simultaneously practicing citizenship by participating in real-world problems.

The following are suggestions on how elementary students can take informed action, but this short list is only the beginning of how students can practice real-world citizenship.

- Write a letter to a local or state official.
- Plan and hold a mock election for another grade level.
- Create community exhibits.
- Participate in community service projects.
- Create posters to hang around the halls of your school.
- Write public service announcements to be read during daily school announcements.
- Create a video to post on the school's social media.
- Write letters of gratitude to members of the military.
- Invite a local politician or school board member to your class.

Another type of civic practice is participating in simulations. Simulations and games allow students to engage in civic roles that are reserved for adults, such as voting, public advocacy, and defending civil rights (Driscoll & McCusker, 2022). For example, after a unit on voting or the election process, students could participate in an in-class voting simulation choosing the next Candy President. Students could participate in each step of the election process, from campaigning to the final vote. Other types of simulations can be found online. One online resource is iCivics (www.icivics.org), which allows students to engage in online simulations related to civic duties of both government officials and citizens.

The classroom-based assessment provides a way for students to demonstrate their content mastery and internalization of enduring understandings. However, engaging in acts of citizenship by doing social studies—through taking informed action or participating in simulations—enables students to transfer these skills to real-world, authentic situations.

Integration Idea
ELA

According to literacy education professor Timothy V. Rasinski (2012), fluency in reading is the bridge between word accuracy and comprehension and should be built "through authentic wide and deep reading practice" (p. 519). One strategy to build fluency is a reader's theater. In a reader's theater, the actors use a script, but there are no costumes or props. The audience visualizes the action as readers perform the play through reading. Fluency is built through repeated readings as students practice the script. After studying the Constitution, civic responsibilities like jury duty, or the roles of citizens, one way to build fluency and provide civic practice is to engage in a reader's theater of courtroom simulations, such as through mock trial scripts found at www.flmd.uscourts.gov/sample-mock-trial-scripts.

Building Your Own Unit

It's time to return to the unit you started building in chapter 1 (page 11) and add the assessment pieces to your four-step planning process template. Figure 2.4 shows an example of step 2 of the four-step planning process for grades K–2.

Topic or Unit:	Veterans Day
Step 1: Making Meaning of Standards	
Standard: D2.His.3.K-2. GENERATE questions about <u>individuals and groups</u> who have shaped a <u>significant historical change</u>.	
Enduring Understanding: Soldiers make sacrifices because they want to protect their country and its citizens.	
Compelling Question: What is a hero?	

Figure 2.4: Step 2 of the four-step planning process example for grades K–2.

continued ▶

Step 2: Creating Assessments
Classroom-Based Assessment: Whole-class discussion leads to drawing a claim; students might draw a picture of a soldier and label it with the term *hero*.
Doing Social Studies: Students will take informed action by writing thank-you letters to local veterans.

Source for standard: NCSS, 2013.

Figure 2.5 shows an example of step 2 of the four-step planning process for grades 3–5.

Topic or Unit:	Veterans Day
Step 1: Making Meaning of Standards	
Standard: D2.His.6.3-5. DESCRIBE how people's <u>perspectives</u> shaped the <u>historical sources</u> they created.	
Enduring Understanding: Our beliefs and values affect our actions.	
Compelling Question: How do people's perspectives influence their decisions?	
Step 2: Creating Assessments	
Classroom-Based Assessment: Students will answer the compelling question using the claims-evidence-reasoning framework in a written paragraph.	
Doing Social Studies: Students will take informed action by writing thank-you letters to local veterans.	

Source for standard: NCSS, 2013.

Figure 2.5: Step 2 of the four-step planning process example for grades 3–5.

Continue building your own social studies unit using the template you started in chapter 1 (page 11). If you would like to transfer everything to a clean template, return to the reproducible "The Four-Step Planning Process Template" (page 128) in appendix A. At this point, complete only step 2, choosing the classroom-based assessment product your students will make as they answer the compelling question using the CER framework, as well as a way students can take informed action and practice citizenship.

Summary

In chapter 1, you learned how to complete the first step of the unit planning process: Making Meaning of Social Studies Standards. In this chapter, you learned about assessments for social studies units built around a compelling question.

First, we looked at how to use classroom-based assessments based on the CER framework, strategies for practicing the skills of claim-evidence-reasoning thinking and writing, and various products students can create to demonstrate their understanding of the content and the compelling question in your unit. Next, we looked at ways to enable students to transfer the enduring understandings they developed into authentic, real-world acts of citizenship by either taking informed action or participating in simulations. In order to support the claims they made in their classroom-based assessments, students will need evidence from sources. Choosing and analyzing primary and secondary sources are covered in chapters 3 (page 47) and 4 (page 81).

CHAPTER 3

Step 3: Choosing and Analyzing Primary Sources

I t's time to imagine again that you are the first-year elementary teacher from the previous chapters. You have chosen and unpacked a standard for your unit, identified an enduring understanding from the standard, crafted a compelling question, and created an assessment. You are now faced with the challenge of teaching the content from the standard and providing experiences for your students to practice social studies skills and processes. However, imagine your district doesn't have a social studies curriculum or adopted resource. You will need to find resources and create activities that will enable your students to interact with these resources. Where do you start?

In this chapter, we will look at step 3 of the four-step planning process: Choosing and Analyzing Primary Sources. We will start by learning about the importance of text sets in social studies. Next, we will dive into what a primary source is and the importance of using them in the elementary classroom, along with a list of online places to find elementary-appropriate sources. We will then examine a set of primary-source analysis historical thinking skills to use with students that includes teacher support in the form of questions, think-alouds, and activities to use while teaching each thinking skill. Then, we will address additional considerations, including how to present sources to students in engaging ways and how to encourage collaboration as students analyze sources. At the end of the chapter, you will find examples of step 3 of the four-step planning process for grades K–2 and grades 3–5 and continue creating your own unit by adding primary sources and analysis strategies to the four-step planning process template you started in chapter 1 (page 11).

Text Sets in Social Studies

In 2016, professors Gina N. Cervetti, Tanya S. Wright, and HyeJin Hwang conducted a research study around conceptually coherent texts and their effect on comprehension. Conceptually coherent texts, also referred to as *text sets*, "are collections of texts tightly focused on a specific topic," writes elementary educator Shannon Garrison (2016). Ideal text sets include "varied genres (fiction, nonfiction, poetry, and so forth) and media (such as blogs, maps, photographs, art, primary-source documents, and audio recordings)" (Garrison, 2016). The study by Cervetti and colleagues (2016) finds a positive effect on comprehension, as students who reviewed text sets were able to recall details, understand the concepts, and explain targeted vocabulary words better than students who read a collection of texts on unrelated topics. These positive effects are echoed by other educational researchers. Authors Meredith Liben and Susan Pimentel (n.d.) ascertain that students build a depth of understanding of concepts as they read through a text set. Language and literacy professor Tanya S. Wright (2021) explains that as students "encounter the same important words that are critical for learning about a concept again and again across the texts . . . this natural repetition supports vocabulary development and knowledge building" (p. 66).

How does this research specifically relate to the work we will do next in building social studies units? You will create text sets when you choose primary and secondary sources for a compelling question. These text sets will be built around coherent topics, concepts, and vocabulary. This thoughtful process is important for building knowledge of enduring understandings in the elementary social studies classroom. As author and educational consultant Beth Pandolpho (2020) states, text sets enable "students to grapple with primary source documents, read fiction and nonfiction texts, glean the wisdom of the ages, and rejoice in the shared experience of stories" (p. 72).

Primary Sources

There are two types of historical sources: (1) primary and (2) secondary. A *primary source* is "an account or record (such as a first-hand account, a contemporaneous news report, a photograph, or an audio or video recording) reflecting direct experience of a thing (such as an historical event) that is being researched or studied" (Primary Source, n.d.). The Library of Congress (n.d.b) defines primary sources as "the raw materials of history—original documents and objects that were created at the time under study." These are different from *secondary sources*, which are defined as "accounts that retell, analyze, or interpret events, usually at a distance of time or place" (Library of Congress, n.d.b).

Figure 3.1 shows a newspaper article about the fundraising for the Statue of Liberty's pedestal, which is an example of a textual primary source.

There are several reasons to use primary sources in your social studies units. Teaching with primary sources brings students close to artifacts and documents from a past time or place (Library of Congress, n.d.b), building "an emotional connection with history" and often providing an opportunity to "critically assess opposing perspectives" to understand what happened and why (iCivics, n.d.). Primary sources, such as photographs, artifacts, and documents, encourage students to ask questions and become curious. Additionally, they encourage inferencing and reasoning with evidence (Library of Congress, n.d.a). But most importantly, primary sources provide historical and often firsthand evidence that students require in order to understand content in a way that can aid them in answering the compelling question. For these reasons, it is important to use primary sources throughout every instructional unit. One lesson about primary sources on one day of the year isn't the goal. We want students to be comfortable analyzing these types of sources and using them as historians on a regular basis.

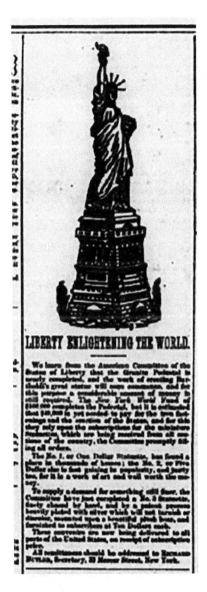

Source: Library of Congress, n.d.a.

Figure 3.1: Example of a primary source, circa 1885.

Sources fulfill different purposes throughout your social studies unit. According to Swan and colleagues (2018), the three instructional purposes of sources are "to spark curiosity, to build knowledge, and to support the development of an argument" (p. 78). In other words, some sources will be used at the beginning of your unit as a hook, other sources will be used to build knowledge about the content, while others provide the evidence needed to answer the compelling question.

Integration Idea
ELA

According to Reading Rockets (n.d.), inferences are based on evidence and reasoning. We make inferences when we figure things out by applying our own knowledge and experiences to questions about our current situation. Developing inferencing skills in ELA leads to better comprehension. A common inference strategy is to teach students to think, "What does the text say?" and "What do I know about this?" and then come up with a "So this means . . ." idea. For example, *the text says the girl has sweaty palms, and I know that my palms sweat when I am nervous, so the girl must be nervous about the situation she is facing.* Developing inferencing skills in ELA also supports inferencing in social studies. When analyzing primary sources, students make inferences when they ask, "What do I see?" and then make connections to their own experiences and reflect on what the source might mean or represent. For example, *there are students sitting in rows at desks in this black-and-white photograph. I know that students today sit at desks in school. This must be a photo of students in a school from a long time ago.* Helping students see the connection between inferencing in ELA and inferencing in social studies primary-source analysis will help them develop this skill across all content areas.

Sometimes one source can fulfill more than one purpose. For example, you might use a photograph to spark students' curiosity about a historical event and use that same photograph to build knowledge about who was involved in that event. Students might also use details from the same photograph as evidence when answering the compelling question. It is important to think about and make a list of the content you want students to learn, as well as the ideas related to the enduring understanding you want them to process before you start looking for sources. This list will enable you to evaluate the usefulness and purpose of the sources you find.

Integration Idea
Science

Opt to include social studies primary sources, secondary sources, or both in the text sets you create for reading, science, or mathematics. For example, let's say that your students are learning about conservation in science. You will more than likely create a text set for this unit that includes pages from your science textbook, articles, and videos. But another text you could use is the NCSS Notable Social Studies Trade Book *The Skydiving Beavers: A True Tale* (Wood, 2017). This beautiful picture book tells the true story of a conservation effort in 1948 by the Idaho Department of Fish and Game to relocate a beaver colony by air-dropping the beavers using parachutes to a new location (Wood, 2017). There are several primary sources you could use to introduce the book or to use with students after reading. You can watch actual video footage of the skydiving beavers (www.skydivingbeavers.com/video.html), look at photographs of the event (Sherriff, 2016), and read a letter from a young girl to a different department, Alaska Fish and Wildlife Service, about another historical event, the Exxon Oil spill (Docsteach.org, n.d.). As a reminder, just reading a social studies text during other content areas is not effective social studies implementation. Practicing the skills of historians is the goal, so be sure to consult this chapter and chapter 4 (page 81) to choose analysis strategies to use with the primary and secondary sources you integrate into other content areas.

Where to Find Primary Sources

According to the NCSS, "The consideration of which sources to use in lesson and unit planning—and specifically primary source documents—is a fundamental practice in good social studies pedagogy" (Waring, 2023, p. v). It is important to be intentional in finding purposeful texts that will provide the evidence that students need to support their claims as they answer the compelling question. According to educational consultant Nancy L. Hennessy (2021), if the development of knowledge is one of our goals, then "the identification of critical understandings and purposeful texts is essential" (p. 46). But where do you find primary sources? The digital world we live in provides students and teachers with access to many sources, both primary and secondary. From the National Archives to virtual museums and online textbook resources, access to primary sources is at your fingertips.

Where do you begin? The first place to look for sources is in your district-adopted resources. This may be textbooks, online subscription programs, or supplemental resources your district has purchased to support your social studies instruction. There may be photographs, document excerpts, or photographs of artifacts in the text that provide ready-to-use primary sources. There are many online resources to help if you do not have resources provided by your district or you are looking for more. Table 3.1 provides some guidance on large-scale, elementary-friendly online resources and the types of content you can find at each site. While there are many sites referenced throughout this book, I do not endorse everything stated or shared on those sites. I encourage you to study and review each one before using it in your classroom. There may be points of view, perspectives, or interpretations of history that you choose not to include.

Remember, you will want to include a variety of primary sources in your unit. The exact number will depend on the length of your unit and the length of time needed to engage with and analyze each source, as well as the availability of sources related to your content topic. It is also acceptable to have multiple sources that cover the same concepts or topics. For long-term retention of words and ideas to occur, students should be exposed to the same vocabulary and concepts for days or weeks (Wexler, 2019). Begin by choosing sources that support your lesson objectives (iCivics, n.d.). You also need to consider the type of information your students will need to build content knowledge and what sources will provide those facts and details. In addition, you need to think about the types of sources students must engage with to answer the compelling question.

Table 3.1: Online Resources for Finding Primary Sources

Online Resource	Types of Content
Library of Congress Primary Source Sets (Library of Congress, n.d.c)	• State-specific collections • U.S. history collections
Library of Congress free to use and reuse (www.loc.gov/free-to-use)	• U.S. history • Holidays • Sports • Science
Chronicling America (https://chroniclingamerica.loc.gov)	• People • Places • Events
Life Magazine photo archive (http://images.google.com/hosted/life)	• People • Places • Events • Sports • Culture • Decades
DocsTeach from the National Archives (www.docsteach.org/documents)	• U.S. history
Smithsonian American Art Museum (https://learninglab.si.edu/org/american-art)	• U.S. history
Digital Inquiry Group: Reading Like a Historian History Lessons (https://inquirygroup.org/history-lessons)	• Modified historical documents
Gilder Lehrman (www.gilderlehrman.org)	• U.S. history
KidCitizen (www.kidcitizen.net)	• Interactive videos of primary sources
Teachinghistory.org (https://teachinghistory.org)	• Primary sources, lessons
Digital Public Library of America (https://dp.la/primary-source-sets)	• Primary sources collections

Figure 3.2 (page 54) provides an example of how to identify the content (based on the standard) and ideas (based on the enduring understanding) and ensure that a source will help you teach that content or idea. Note that choosing and analyzing secondary sources will be covered in chapter 4 (page 81).

Content or Idea	Source
Define the word *veteran* and understand that veterans can be everyday people in our communities.	Picture Book: *What Is a Veteran, Anyway?* by Robert C. Snyder (2016) (secondary source) Picture Book: *Veterans: Heroes in Our Neighborhood* by Valerie Pfundstein (2012) (secondary source)
Give examples of the sacrifices veterans make because they want to protect their country and its citizens.	Photograph: Soldiers Carry a Wounded Comrade Through a Swamp www.docsteach.org/documents/document/soldiers-carry-wounded (primary source) Photograph: American Reinforcements Arriving on the French Coast www.docsteach.org/documents/document/dday-american-reinforcements (primary source) Picture Book: *Proud as a Peacock, Brave as a Lion* by Jane Barclay (2009) (secondary source)
Explain how communities honor veterans' sacrifices.	Photograph: Veterans Day Ceremony at the Vietnam Veterans Memorial www.docsteach.org/documents/document/veterans-day-ceremony-memorial (primary source) Picture book: *The Wall* by Eve Bunting (2001) (secondary source)

Figure 3.2: Matching content and ideas to sources for a K–2 unit about veterans.

Primary Source Analysis Strategies

After choosing your sources, you need to consider how students will analyze them to extract the knowledge, vocabulary, and concepts needed to show mastery of the standard by answering the compelling question. According to the NCSS, when planning social studies lessons, "it is essential for teachers to include not only content but also the skills students are expected to perform when addressing that specific content" (Waring, 2023, p. 103). The skill of analyzing primary sources will need to be explicitly modeled and taught if students are going to use the content within sources to build arguments.

In Digital Inquiry Group's (n.d.) "Reading Like a Historian" lessons for middle and high school, the organization proposes approaching primary sources using the historical reading skills of sourcing, contextualizing, close reading, and corroborating. I have adapted these skills to make them applicable to elementary

Integration Idea
Science and ELA

The lists of where to find primary and secondary sources in this chapter (table 3.1, page 53) and chapter 4 (table 4.1, page 86) are a great place to begin curating your text sets for social studies, as well as science and ELA. Several resources in these lists contain already curated text sets to save time as you begin planning. These text sets include visual, digital, and traditional texts. Don't be afraid to use texts that at first glance may seem difficult for your students. You can scaffold understanding of the text through reading it aloud and planning intentional discussions. According to education writer Natalie Wexler (2024), "Students' listening comprehension exceeds their reading comprehension through about age thirteen, on average" (pp. ix–x). "That means," she explains, that lower elementary grade learners "can take in more sophisticated concepts and vocabulary through listening than through their own reading" (Wexler, 2024, p. x).

school and refer to them as *historical thinking skills*, as students will be using them with both written and visual sources. Table 3.2 (page 56) provides an explanation of each skill, and the sections following will detail how to use that skill with lower elementary grade students. One or more of these skills should be used with every primary source students analyze. If you are working with lower elementary grade students, or upper elementary grade students who are unfamiliar with primary source analysis, you will want to explicitly teach each skill before beginning your first unit.

Another tip is to visit the Digital Inquiry Group website (https://inquiry group.org), where you can freely download historical thinking skills posters. The posters include each of the skills and related questions to ask. You can shrink these posters down to trading card size, and students can use them as they analyze sources.

Now let's take a closer look at these four historical thinking skills with a special emphasis on strategies for close reading. The chapter will then wrap up with a section on using analysis charts and additional considerations for analyzing primary sources.

Table 3.2: Historical Thinking Skills

Historical Thinking Skill	Explanation
Sourcing	Determining the type of source, who wrote or created the source, and when it was created and asking why someone would create this type of source
Contextualizing	Thinking about how, when, and where a source was created might affect its origination
Close reading	Reading to determine the author's perspective and claim
Corroborating	Comparing and contrasting this source to other sources

Source: Adapted from Digital Inquiry Group, n.d.

Sourcing

Sourcing includes determining the type of primary source (for example, a letter, photograph, or document), who wrote or created the source, when it was created, and why someone might create this type of source. This information will be important as students try to make sense of the source during close reading. Often, this information is found in the source's bibliographic information. Even though the name of who wrote or created the source is provided, you may need to provide additional background information about a person unfamiliar to your students. Applying this skill should take about three to five minutes, and you might introduce it like this:

> Today we are going to look at a primary source from the past. It will help us gather evidence as we try to answer the compelling question for this unit. The first thing we should do when looking at primary sources is a historical thinking skill called **sourcing**. We do this by asking and answering the following questions.
>
> • What type of source is it?
>
> • Who created it?
>
> • When was it created?
>
> • Why would someone create this type of source?
>
> We will use the source's bibliographic data to help us answer these questions.

Regarding the last bulleted question, it is important to note that your students aren't trying to figure out why a person created this particular source. Instead, they should be trying to determine why people create different types of sources in a more general sense. Author and school librarian Tom Bober (2019) provides several examples in his book *Elementary Educator's Guide to Primary Sources*:

> Why would someone write in a diary? Diary entries may be written to keep track of events or to write down information they do not want to share with others. Why do people make maps? Maybe a map is created to show others how a space is organized or laid out. Why do people write a news story? More than likely, it is written to inform people. (p. 60)

Both Bober (2019) and the Digital Inquiry Group (n.d.) point out the importance of having students think about the reliability of sources. Although elementary students will almost always have their teacher provide reliable sources, eventually, students will be asked to find their own sources as they enter middle and high school.

When working with lower elementary grade students, you may need to tell students the type of primary source they are analyzing if they are unfamiliar with that type of document or image. You may also need to read the bibliographic information to them and model how to use it to answer the sourcing questions. Lower elementary grade students may be unfamiliar with people or events that upper elementary grade students already have knowledge about, so you may need to spend some time building background knowledge by sharing picture books or short videos on those topics.

Contextualizing

Contextualizing is thinking about how, when, and where a source was created might affect its creation. Contextualizing is also about collecting information to use when close reading, so it should take only three to five minutes. You might introduce this skill like this:

> *Another historical thinking skill is called* **contextualizing**. *This skill helps us figure out what was going on around the same time as the source's creation and how that might affect the source's perspective. We do this by asking and answering the following questions.*
>
> • *Is this from today or long ago?*
>
> • *What do we know about this time period?*
>
> • *How did the period in which this was created affect why or how someone might have created it?*
>
> *To help answer these questions, you might think about what you already know about the details we discovered during sourcing.*

If students have limited background knowledge about a time period at the beginning of your unit, you may need to build knowledge by showing a short video or by reading a picture book or short informational text about the topic, person, or event. If this is a source being used later in your unit, you may need to remind students of what they have already learned about the topic, person, or event to help them contextualize the new primary source. With lower elementary grade learners, you may want to focus on the first part of contextualizing: deciding whether the source is from today or long ago and discussing how students know. This will begin to build students' ability to use evidence to support claims.

Close Reading

Scholars often use the term *close reading* in the context of literary criticism. Per the fourth edition of the online Oxford Dictionary of Literary Terms (Oxford University Press, n.d.), close reading is:

> A term commonly applied to the detailed analysis of a literary text, usually a short poem or prose excerpt. In a modern tradition . . . the close reader typically attempts to account for and justify the presence of all the text's features of sound and sense, usually detecting sonic correspondences such as internal rhyme and alliteration, along with ambiguities of meaning, and the complex deployment of rhetorical figures, all integrated into a formal unity.

This definition works for the type of close reading done in an English class. But the type of close reading used by historians has a different purpose. According to educator and researcher Timothy Shanahan (2013) ". . . Historians read very differently than literary critics—they would be interested in the sources of [the document] (what led to it, what shaped it), and what its implications were." In other words, historians look not only at the text inside the source, but they also look at what was happening during that time outside the source to make meaning of the text. "Close reading in one tradition examines the language within the document without concern for its external connections, and in the other close reading requires the connection of a document with its context, etc." (Shanahan, 2013). Shanahan (2012) simplified the definition of close reading when he said it is "an intensive analysis of a text in order to come to terms with what it says, how it says it, and what it means."

This is the work students will be doing in social studies as they analyze primary sources and begin to take a closer look at the details within the source. For written texts, these details might include the vocabulary, word choice, or specific ideas. For visual sources, these details might include thinking about the people, places, or events in the source through the five senses. Close reading primary sources is the heart of the analysis process; therefore, students will linger here much longer than in the previous skills. Close reading can take anywhere from fifteen to sixty minutes depending on your students' experience with this skill as well as the type of source you are examining. For example, a visual source like a photograph may take only fifteen minutes to close read, but a longer textual source—a news article or document such as the Declaration of Independence—may take an hour.

Remember that you will model and complete each of these skills with your students multiple times before having them work on these skills independently. With lower elementary grade students, all close reading may be completed as a whole class. With upper elementary grade students, you might model how to close read the first part of the text, have them work in pairs to complete another part of the text, and then decide if they will continue working in pairs or if they are ready to work on close reading independently. The following is one way you can introduce this skill.

> Another historical thinking skill that historians use is called **close reading** *the source. This means we are going to read or look at this source intensely and see whether we can find details to help us make connections to our compelling question.*

When using the previous skills (sourcing and contextualizing), you would guide students through a short series of questions. Close reading goes beyond a few questions, since the goal is a deep analysis of the source's ideas and content. The following are some strategies you can use to help your students closely read various types of sources. They are divided into two categories: (1) strategies for close reading visual sources and (2) strategies for close reading text-based sources. Visual sources are a good starting point if you work with lower elementary grade students or if analyzing primary sources is new to your students. Students don't have to struggle with difficult vocabulary or reading levels, and visual sources are often more appealing.

Strategies for Close Reading Visual Sources

Visual sources include photographs, paintings, drawings, sculptures, and architecture. There are several benefits of using visual sources that extend beyond the social studies classroom. Visual sources develop students' ability to generate inferences (Hennessy, 2021) and are very accessible to a variety of student learners and students learning English as an additional language (Waring, 2023). In addition, analyzing visual sources develops *visual literacy*, which Waring (2023) defines as "the capability to read, write, comprehend, and generate visual images" (p. 179). Visual literacy is important in a world where visual images bombard us constantly because it builds students' ability to think critically and understand how pictures affect them.

Close reading visual primary sources requires students to look at the details and focus on an activity for an extended length of time. This is not always easy, especially for lower elementary grade students. Anne Savage (as cited in Wesson, 2011b) of the Library of Congress offers suggestions on how to get students to focus in on the details within an image, whether using one small part of the picture (as in the zoom in strategy, see page 61) or when looking at the whole image (as in the thinking routines strategy, see page 61). These suggestions include presenting students with:

- binoculars or magnifying glasses
- frames of cardboard with a square cut in the middle
- two L-shaped pieces of cardboard
- a sheet of paper held in front of an LCD projector to capture a section of the image
- a highlighted area on an interactive whiteboard (Wesson, 2011b)

These suggestions might just bring a renewed sense of excitement to your primary source analysis if your students are struggling to notice the details or lack the stamina to stick with close reading images. The following sections describe the ten visual analysis strategies and activities (Waring, 2023).

Visual Thinking

This strategy from Waring (2023) uses a simple series of questions to encourage students to discuss the visual image or artifact they are close reading. The teacher can ask:

- "What is going on in this picture?"
- "What do you see that makes you say that?"
- "What more can you find?" (Waring, 2023, p. 179)

These questions "stimulate student discussions" when analyzing visual images or artifacts (Waring, 2023, p. 179). This is a good strategy to use with lower elementary grade students or with students who have never analyzed visual primary sources before because it can be a whole-group discussion. It provides prompts for what students should be thinking about when they analyze sources independently in the future.

Thinking Routines

Project Zero, an organization housed at the Harvard Graduate School of Education and founded to conduct research on education and the arts, provides many visual *thinking routines* students can use as they analyze images or artwork (www.pz.harvard.edu/thinking-routines). Project Zero's (2022) thinking routines provide a predictable structure with the purpose of revealing students' thinking using questions and discussion. For example, in the see-think-wonder strategy, students answer three questions as they analyze images or artwork: What do you see? What does this make you think about? and What does it make you wonder? (Project Zero, 2022). This strategy gets students to look closely at sources and to start making inferences about what they think is going on. This strategy is a good choice if you are trying to hook students into the lesson. Because all students can answer those three questions at varying degrees of depth, this strategy works with all K–5 students.

Zoom In

This strategy inspires curiosity by taking a primary source and revealing parts of it before the whole. As the source is revealed one part at a time, students discover they have new observations, reflections, and questions (Library of Congress, n.d.c). Begin by dividing a visual source into several parts. Students answer the following questions as each part of the source is revealed.

- What objects do you see?
- Is this picture old or new?
- What do you think this might be? (Library of Congress, n.d.c)

As more parts are revealed, students will revise previous reflections and generate questions for what they want to know by thinking about additional questions.

- What new information do you have?
- What do you think is happening? (Library of Congress, n.d.c)

After the entire picture has been revealed, you can lead a discussion about what students know about the history, event, or people in the picture. As a culminating activity, students can create a caption for the picture. Educator Tina M. Ellsworth recommends a variation in which students create a caption for the image as each part is revealed (T. Ellsworth, personal communication, February 16, 2024). At the end of the zoom in, students can see how their captions changed over time to reveal the details of the image that will enable them to write their final caption. Sometimes this strategy is referred to as *quartering* because the image is divided into four parts. Visit https://sites.msudenver.edu/tpswesternregion/how-to-create-a-zoom-in-inquiry-activity for detailed directions on how to create a zoom-in inquiry using PowerPoint or Google Slides.

Consider using the jigsaw strategy for upper elementary grade students; it is similar to zoom in, but students do part of it on their own. In this strategy, each student in a small group would be given one part of the picture. Each student would answer the questions about their part, then share their thinking with the group. Students would then discuss what they think is going on in the picture without showing their individual pieces. Once students have made a prediction, they put their pieces together to check their thinking while also discussing what new information they have when the pieces are put together.

Caption Matching

This strategy encourages students to observe the details in an image as they try to match the captions that go with each visual primary source. To use this strategy, collect a variety of visual primary sources, including photographs, artwork, or artifacts related to your topic that include captions. Separate the captions from the primary sources and give each small group of students a set of images with a set of captions. Students must work together to match each caption with the correct primary source. For example, when teaching about the roles of the president during a government unit, you could have a stack of photographs of the president doing various tasks (giving a speech, meeting with foreign leaders, or signing bills into laws) and students must match the caption to the correct photograph. Follow up the activity with a discussion about what students learned from the captions and details in the primary sources. For lower elementary grade students, you may need to read the captions to the students one at a time, drawing attention to the action words and descriptive phrases so that students can make meaning of the captions before trying to match them. You might also provide every student with the collection of primary sources, read a caption, and have students hold up the primary source they think matches. Upper elementary grade students can write their own captions for the photographs. They could do this as a hook to the unit and then return to their captions and revise them based on their new learning at the end of a unit.

Thirty-Second Look

Stacie Moats (as cited in Wesson, 2011a) of the Library of Congress offers this strategy that encourages students to look closely at the small details within an image. Give students thirty seconds to look at an image, such as a photograph, artwork, or artifact, and challenge them to memorize as many details as possible during that time without talking to one another or taking notes. Then hide the image and have students individually record everything they remember about the image. Finally, lead a whole-class discussion to compare and discuss their observations, then show the image again. As an extension of this strategy, you can have students discuss what new details they notice the second time and how it changes their thinking about what is going on in the picture.

Hide-and-Seek

In this strategy, also from Moats (as cited in Wesson, 2011a), students study a small part of an image individually and then collectively share their thinking as a group to build on one another's ideas. First, Moats recommends show-ing students an image and telling them to "pretend to be as small as a fly and find a secret hiding place" in the image (Wesson, 2011a). After students have secretly chosen their hiding place, you act as the seeker by identifying possible hiding places in the image. When you identify a student's hiding place, they raise their hand to indicate they've been found. Students can share what they see, hear, touch, or smell in their hiding place.

This strategy works best with lower elementary grade students. To modify for upper elementary grade students, have students work in pairs after teaching them the strategy. One partner gives clues using sensory details about where they are hiding, and the other partner tries to guess where they are in the image.

News Report

This strategy works best with pictures that have people in them. Working in a small group, students generate a list of questions a news reporter might ask the people in the photograph. For example:

- What are you doing?
- Why are you in this particular place?
- Why are you smiling, frowning, or laughing?

Students work together to answer the questions based on details in the picture. After working in small groups, students share their thinking in a whole-group discussion. You can record each group's thinking on a class chart. At the end, lead a discussion about where and when the picture was taken, what the people in the picture are doing, and how the picture helps students understand the time or event they are studying.

Jumping In

This activity and the two that follow are specific to close reading a specific type of visual source—portraits. These activities involve analysis of a portrait to learn more about the person in the artwork, as well as what life was like during that time (Bell, 2016). Students visualize themselves jumping into the portrait. They explain where they are in the portrait, answer questions related to the five senses, and explain what their observations may say about the person in the portrait and the time in which they lived.

Strike a Pose

In this strategy, students pose like the person in the portrait. They think about what it would feel like to sit that way, wear the clothes the person is wearing, and live during that time. Consider using props like those in the portrait so lower elementary grade students can more easily mimic what they see. For upper elementary grade students, if possible, find portraits of the person at different stages in life. Students can work in pairs to converse with each other as their *young self* and their *old self*, comparing their thinking from each stage of life. It is important to note that you would never want to ask students to pose in uncomfortable or sensitive situations, such as a slave auction. The purpose of this strategy is to take a portrait of a single person posing for a photograph or painting and recreate the pose to encourage student thinking about that time period.

What Would You Ask

Students generate a list of questions they would ask the person in the portrait in this strategy. This encourages them to think like the person and about the time in which the person lived. Students can then try to answer as many questions as possible using the portrait and their questions to guide their reading of secondary sources about the person.

Strategies for Close Reading Text Sources

Here are four strategies to use when close reading text-based sources. This includes written documents but can also include interview transcripts. As mentioned earlier, it is best to begin primary source analysis with lower elementary grade learners by using visual images, but that doesn't mean you can't use text-based sources with them as well. Bober (2019) suggests using shorter primary source texts, including "newspaper headlines, or consider choosing a small portion of a full primary source text" (p. 42). This might include a short paragraph from a letter, newspaper article, or document instead of the entire text.

Student-Generated Questions

Students comprehend information better when they ask and answer their own questions about a text than when answering only teacher-generated questions. Education authors Judith C. Hochman and Natalie Wexler (2017) write that developing questions also "encourages students to think about the important features in text" while fostering close reading skills, helping students home in on the key parts of questions, and encouraging them to practice using vocabulary (p. 36).

According to nonprofit educational organization Right Question Institute (n.d.), the Question Formulation Technique is a structure for generating and improving questions to allow students to "think critically, feel greater power and self-efficacy, and become more confident and ready to participate in civic life." An elementary-friendly version of this technique from coauthors LeAnn Nickelsen and Melissa Dickson (2022) is called "question generation PIP (produce, improve, prioritize)" (p. 252). While reading a text-based primary source, students write questions about the text in the margin or on sticky notes. After reading, students share their questions with their group and identify questions as closed or open ended. This is the first step of the PIP strategy: produce questions. Next, students rewrite closed-ended questions as open-ended questions. This is the second step of the PIP strategy: improve questions. Finally, students reach consensus on their top two or three most important questions. This is the third step of the PIP strategy: prioritize questions. Students can research their questions, or you can make those questions a reading focus as you read other sources during the unit.

This strategy works well with text-based primary sources, such as documents, diary entries, newspaper articles, or letters. For lower elementary grade students, you can read the source to them and then record their questions, improve their questions for them, and lead students in a whole-class discussion using the questions they want to learn more about. For upper elementary grade students, you can model the strategy by completing it as a whole group for the first source and then have students work in groups to complete the strategy for another source.

Figure 3.3 (page 66) contains an example of the first two steps of the question-generation PIP strategy for a close reading of the First Amendment of the Bill of Rights. Note that the Improve Questions column for the last question is blank because it's already an open-ended question. After completing these steps, each group would prioritize the most important questions and circle those on the chart.

Questions	Open or Closed?	Improve Questions
What is a right?	Closed	How do we determine rights?
What is a petition?	Closed	Why do people write petitions?
What does it mean to assemble?	Closed	What are examples of people assembling?
Why are there five parts to the First Amendment?	Open	

Figure 3.3: Example of the question-generation PIP strategy for a close reading of the First Amendment of the Bill of Rights.

Annotation

The second strategy for close reading text-based primary sources is annotation. Social studies educator and researcher Chauncey Monte-Sano (2018) explains, "Annotating involves highlighting, underlining, and making marginal notes while reading a document." Annotating can be used on visual sources, as well as text-based sources like historical documents, newspapers, letters, or diary entries. Educators Robin J. Fogarty, Gene M. Kerns, and Brian M. Pete (2021) indicate that annotation allows the reader to have a conversation with the author and with their own thinking, which has been shown to improve engagement and comprehension.

For lower elementary grade students, keep the annotations simple and do only two or three at a time. For example, students could put a smiley face next to parts of a visual image that they already know something about or a question mark next to confusing parts of the image. For upper elementary grade students, you can allow the students to come up with their own annotation symbols. For example, students might suggest putting question marks next to confusing words or phrases, exclamation marks next to words or phrases that seem important, and stars next to words or phrases that connect to previous learning. A whole-group discussion should follow once students annotate the text. You might choose to define confusing vocabulary and answer questions or use these annotations as a guide for further research and learning about the topic.

Word-Phrase-Sentence

According to Project Zero (2019), word-phrase-sentence is "a routine for capturing the essence of a text." After reading the primary source, students individually record three things.

1. A word that seems important

2. A phrase that seems powerful

3. A sentence that captures the main idea of the text

Students then discuss in small groups their word, phrase, and sentence. They explain why they made their choices and then compare with their group members' choices. A discussion about common themes and ideas can lead to a summary of the source and its significance.

Ranking

This strategy is best done in small groups and helps students extract the most important concepts or ideas from a written primary source. Each group reads the same primary source, chooses the three to five most important sentences, and writes each of those sentences on its own sheet of paper. Each person in the group holds a different sentence. Then, students stand shoulder to shoulder to show how they would rank the sentences in importance. After all groups have ranked their sentences, groups share with the whole class to defend their claims. The whole-class discussion leads to a summary of the most important concepts or ideas for students to understand. A tip for this strategy is to give each group of students the ace, two, three, four, and five card from a deck of playing cards. They write their sentences on sticky notes and put each sticky note on the card that matches their ranking. For lower elementary grade students, give them only three cards, and allow them to write important words instead of sentences or to draw pictures. Figure 3.4 shows an example of ranking using playing cards.

Figure 3.4: Example of ranking using playing cards.

Corroborating

In the previous sections, you learned about the first three historical thinking skills: sourcing, contextualizing, and close reading. The information gleaned from the previous skills sets students up for the fourth and final historical thinking skill, corroborating. *Corroborating* is comparing and contrasting the information found in multiple sources. Corroboration is important because often one source won't provide all the information about an event, person, or topic, and some sources don't include the voice or perspective of every group involved in the event. According to Waring (2023), "Historical thinking that promotes corroboration can successfully integrate content from textbooks with primary and secondary sources" (p. 102). To get a complete picture, multiple sources and multiple kinds of sources are needed.

Start with simple questions to practice corroborating with lower elementary grade students, such as, How are these two sources the same, and how are they different? You will want upper elementary grade students to use more than two sources and go beyond just a comparison. This could include questions like, What do other sources say? Do they agree? Why might they agree or disagree? You might introduce this skill by saying:

> Now that we have analyzed multiple sources about our topic, let's think about how the information in the sources is the same and how it is different. Do the sources agree? And if not, why might they have different information?

You can record students' thinking and reflections in a Venn diagram that compares the details in each source, or you may want to do a deeper analysis with a comparison matrix, which compares multiple characteristics or ideas about two or more sources. Figure 3.5 shows a comparison matrix that could be used to compare two different written accounts by participants of the Boston Tea Party.

Questions	Account 1	Account 2
How does the writer describe the events leading up to the Boston Tea Party?		
How does the writer describe the mood or tone of the Boston Tea Party?		
How does the writer describe the actions of the participants of the Boston Tea Party?		

Figure 3.5: Comparison matrix for the Boston Tea Party.

Analysis Charts

Each of the primary source analysis strategies that was previously discussed was specific to close reading skills. Analysis charts guide students through a step-by-step analysis of the source with a series of questions using all the historical thinking skills at one time instead of each skill separately. These questions will help students think about what they see in the source, who created the source, why the source was created, and what the source was used for. These graphic organizers can be simple charts that students or teachers create digitally or on chart paper. If you are a first-year teacher or new to primary source analysis, these charts are a great first step because they require little planning and walk you and your students through the process of historical thinking and primary source analysis step-by-step.

Daniel M. Argentar and colleagues (2021) recommend using a graphic organizer before, during, and after reading the primary source. Before reading, students identify the type of document, author, date creation, and source of the document. During reading, students think about the style or language of the document, point of view, and key vocabulary words. After reading, students consider the main idea, impact of the document, questions raised, and further research students could conduct. All this information can be recorded in an analysis chart, either on chart paper as a whole group or on a graphic organizer completed by small groups or pairs. To save time, teachers can also use premade charts that can be found online. National Archives (www.archives.gov /education/lessons/worksheets) has student-friendly analysis charts for many different types of primary sources, including photographs, documents, artifacts, and artwork. Figure 3.6 (page 70) shows a sample completed analysis chart for analyzing a photograph.

The Library of Congress also has a free primary source analysis tool that asks students to observe, reflect, and question as they analyze primary sources (Library of Congress, n.d.d).

When working with lower elementary grade students, consider enlarging the analysis chart or graphic organizer and filling in the responses from the students as you work as a whole group to analyze the source. After modeling and completing several analysis charts together, upper elementary grade students can complete the charts in pairs or small groups.

Analyze a Photograph		
Meet the photo:	**Observe its parts:**	**Try to make sense of it:**
What do you see?	Circle what you see in the photo.	Who do you think took this photo?
People, flags, flowers, people wearing military clothes	People Objects (Both)	*A newspaper reporter or someone at the ceremony*
Is the photo . . .	What are the objects used in the photo?	List something that helps you prove where it was taken.
☐ Black and white	*The flag is for saying the Pledge of Allegiance, the flowers are for the ceremony*	*The caption gave me the information.*
☑ Color		
Is there a caption?	Write two words that describe the photo.	Why do you think the photo was taken?
☑ Yes	*serious and remembering*	*To remember the ceremony*
☐ No		How does this photo compare to modern times?
If so, what does the caption tell you?		*It is similar to now because we dress like these people.*
This photograph shows a Veterans Day ceremony at the Vietnam Veterans Memorial in Washington, DC.		
Use it as historical evidence:		
Where do you think we could find out more information about the people or objects in the photo?		
We could learn more by visiting the library and reading books about Veterans Day.		

Source: Adapted from National Archives, n.d.

Figure 3.6: Sample analysis chart for analyzing a photograph.

Additional Considerations for Primary Sources

After you have chosen activities to help your students with each of the historical thinking skills (sourcing, contextualizing, close reading, and corroborating), you will want to consider two additional questions: (1) How will you present the primary sources to your students? and (2) How will students collaborate as they analyze the sources?

Integration Idea
Science

Primary sources encompass all content areas, not just social studies. For example, you can practice the four historical thinking skills outlined in this chapter when using primary sources related to events, concepts, and ideas in science. When studying sound waves, you could look for primary sources about the telephone, like this drawing by Alexander Graham Bell found at the Library of Congress (www.loc.gov/resource/magbell.27300105). When learning about weather, you could use this Weather Forecasting collection of primary sources from the Library of Congress (www.loc.gov/classroom-materials/weather-forecasting). Spending a few extra minutes searching for primary sources related to your science units enables you to practice the historical thinking skills (sourcing, contextualizing, close reading, and corroborating) across your day.

Primary Sources—Presentation

After considering the various sources you will use and the purposes they fulfill in the unit (for example, hooking the students, providing background information, or building vocabulary and content knowledge), you will need to think about when and how you will present the sources to your students in the instructional sequence. Sometimes you will want to present one source at a time because you may be using one source at the beginning of the unit, one during the unit, and one at the end of the unit. Other times, you will want to present several at once so that students can begin to build a big picture of the event, person, or idea. The following sections contain presentation ideas that can build excitement and engagement as your students interact with multiple sources at a time.

Historical Scene Investigation

Historical scene investigations set up the primary sources as evidence in a historical mystery. Students act as history detectives to collect evidence to try to solve the mystery. This presentation idea is based on the Historical Scene Investigation Project, which was originally created as a way for teachers to use primary sources in their history classes (Teachinghistory.org, n.d.). Designed for middle school and high school students, many of the investigations in the project were not accessible for elementary students. The following are some adaptations I have made so you can use this structure in your elementary classroom.

To prepare for your investigation, you will need to pick a historical event that has a question for students to investigate. Figure 3.7 shows possible questions for investigation related to various social studies topics.

Topic	Possible Questions for Investigation
The Lost Colony of Roanoke	What happened to the Lost Colony of Roanoke?
American Revolution	Was justice served at the Boston Massacre?
American Revolution	Who fired the first shots at the battles of Lexington and Concord?
Immigration	Did immigrants achieve the American Dream?

Figure 3.7: Historical scene investigation questions for various topics.

Next, you will need to create a case file that introduces the investigation by providing the necessary historical background information your students will need. You can type this up and put it in a folder labeled *Top Secret*. Then, collect the historical sources (primary and secondary sources) and put them in envelopes labeled *Top Secret Evidence Envelopes*.

Now it's time to start the investigation. Begin by telling students that they are historical detectives solving a historical mystery. They will be provided with all the necessary evidence to crack the case and answer the question. As students analyze the evidence (primary and secondary sources), you will want to have them record their thoughts in an evidence log—a graphic organizer they complete as they analyze the sources. Figure 3.8 shows an example evidence log for the topic *the Lost Colony of Roanoke*.

	Evidence #1	Evidence #2	Evidence #3
What is the historical source?			
What is the source date and who is the author, if known?			
Describe details in the source related to the event.			

	Evidence #1	Evidence #2	Evidence #3
Which theory or theories of the Lost Colony does the source seem to support?			
Which theory or theories, if any, does the source seem to refute?			

Figure 3.8: Example of an evidence log for the Lost Colony of Roanoke historical scene investigation.

To further engage your students, have the evidence (primary and secondary sources) laid out and surrounded with crime scene tape (easily found and purchased on the internet) when students come into class for the day. Figure 3.9 shows how you might set up your historical scene investigation.

Figure 3.9: Historical scene investigation setup.

You can also provide magnifying glasses for students to use as they analyze the evidence, allowing them to feel like real detectives.

Another great resource for finding already-prepared historical scene investigations is the Private i History Detectives lessons from iCivics (www.icivics .org/products/privatei). This site provides the primary sources and materials needed, as well as PowerPoints or Google Slides, to guide students through the historical investigations.

Story Before a Story

This presentation idea encourages students to try to tell the story of a historical event before they learn about it by studying a collection of related primary sources (T. Ellsworth, personal communication, March 27, 2023). Provide students with a collection of primary sources related to the event and guide them in analyzing them. After, have students try to tell the story based on information in the sources. After coming up with their story, students generate a list of questions they still have that the sources have not answered. Then, read a picture book or informational text about the event. Lead a discussion as to whether students' stories were accurate and how their thinking has changed. This is also a good time to practice the corroborating historical thinking skill (page 68) by asking students to think about whether or not the information in the sources and the text was similar or different. Figure 3.10 is a graphic organizer students can use as they build their story before a story. You can return to the graphic organizer after learning more to correct students' initial thoughts.

What story do these primary sources tell?	
Who is in the story?	How do you know?
Where does the story take place?	How do you know?
When does the story take place?	How do you know?
What is the story?	How do you know?

Figure 3.10: Story before a story graphic organizer.

Sunken Ship

This presentation idea works for primary sources related to topics that involve the movement of people or ideas across the ocean. To set up the primary sources for a sunken ship, first create the outline of a sunken ship on the floor using tape and create a grid within the ship. Figure 3.11 shows an example of the outline.

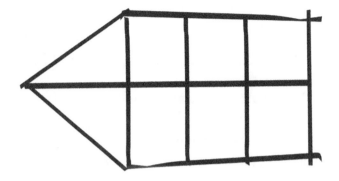

Figure 3.11: Sunken ship outline example.

Put an artifact (either the actual artifact or an image) in each grid square. Since students will need to analyze all the sources, you will want multiple copies of each source in each grid space. You will probably need around eight grid spaces for a class of twenty-four if students are working in pairs. Students "dive" to the bottom of the ocean to retrieve the artifact and then analyze it with their partner using a primary source analysis strategy. Students return to the ship, return their artifact, collect another artifact, and continue this process until they have analyzed all of them.

This presentation idea works well at the beginning of a unit to help students build background knowledge or for generating questions about the topic. It can also be used in the middle of a unit after students have been introduced to a topic and you want them to learn more about a specific aspect of that topic. For example, when introducing a unit on immigration, students could analyze artifacts of items immigrants brought with them to try to determine who was on the ship, where they came from, and why they were on the ship. After students have learned about different groups who immigrated to America during the unit, you may want them to analyze artifacts that reveal reasons for immigration. Figure 3.12 (page 76) gives a suggested list of content topics and related questions you might have students answer after their sunken ship experience.

Topic	Question to Answer
Early Exploration	What were the Europeans' motives for exploration?
Thirteen Colonies	What were the colonists' motives for coming to the colonies?
Economics	Why do countries import and export goods?
Immigration	What were the motives of immigrants coming to America?

Figure 3.12: Sunken ship topics and questions.

Gallery Walk or Rotation Stations

This presentation idea works well when you want students to analyze several sources at a time, but they don't meet any of the characteristics of the previous ideas. For example, when learning about the Bill of Rights, you aren't studying a specific historical story, there is no mystery involved, and students don't need to dive to a sunken ship! So, you can use a gallery walk, sometimes called rotation stations, to present your sources. In this strategy, each source is taped to a large piece of chart paper and each piece of chart paper is hung around the room. Students will travel in pairs or small groups to complete an activity at each station. You might have discussion questions about each source if there are specific details you want the students to learn. You may have them generate questions they have about the sources and record them on the chart paper, or you may choose to have students use one of the analysis strategies from this chapter at each rotation. In the end, students will use the information they gather at the stations to generate or answer questions, corroborate sources, or build background knowledge. Depending on how much time each station takes, you may be able to have students complete all the stations in one day or spread them out over several days.

Primary Sources—Collaboration

After all the planning that has gone into choosing primary sources and setting students up for successful analysis, it can be very disheartening when one student takes over the conversation or several students sit and let others do all the work. Because we want all students involved in the analysis process, you must also spend time planning how the students will work together in small groups. One important benefit of small groups is the discussion that takes place among group members. Discussion in small groups allows students to construct knowledge; deepen their understanding of that knowledge; and become stronger readers, writers, and communicators (Novak & Slattery, 2017). There are also specific benefits to working in small groups within the context of social studies. According to TeachingWorks Resource Library (n.d.):

> The core work of inquiry typically happens in small groups where students can examine sources and other materials, explore compelling questions and problems with one another, discover new ideas, and develop and test their thinking. The opportunities for talk in small groups is essential to sensemaking, language learning, and engagement in inquiry.

The cooperative learning strategy works well in small groups to encourage discussion. This instructional model allows students to discuss complex ideas and opinions about primary sources (Waring, 2023). According to renowned psychology and education author Spencer Kagan (1994), *cooperative learning* involves small heterogeneous groups of students who work together to accomplish a shared goal. Cooperative learning is done in either pairs or groups of three to four. The power of cooperative learning is that each student in the group has a clearly defined role, so all students are responsible for the group's success through equal participation. Table 3.3 provides some cooperative learning strategies that can be used with small groups or pairs as students analyze primary sources.

Table 3.3: Effective Cooperative Learning Strategies to Use With Primary Source Analysis

Cooperative Learning Strategy and Grouping Structure	Description
Expert Groups (Groups of four)	Put students into groups of four. Then give each student in each group a number from 1 to 4. All the ones meet in a group, all the twos meet in a group, and so on. Each "expert" group now receives a different primary or secondary source to analyze using an analysis strategy. Students then return to their original group to share out their analysis and observations.
Teammates Consult (Groups of four)	Provide students with their own copies of the same primary or secondary source. Have each student team gather and place a large cup in the center of the group. Students begin by placing their pencils in the cup. With pencils resting, they discuss their answers to the first question or part of the analysis strategy. When everyone in the group is ready, students remove their pencils from the cup and quietly record their answers. They then repeat this process for the remaining questions (Dotson, 2001).

continued ▶

Cooperative Learning Strategy and Grouping Structure	Description
Think-Pair-Share (Partners)	Pose a question from an analysis strategy and invite students to think for a bit about their responses. Then, pair students up so they can discuss their ideas with partners. Finally, have students share their ideas with the larger group (Lyman, 1981).
	For upper elementary grade students, require them to share their partners' thinking instead of their own ideas to develop listening skills.
Read-Write-Pair-Share (Partners)	Similar to think-pair-share, students will first read an article (or primary source), write their thinking about the source (open ended or in response to a prompt from the teacher), and then pair and share with their partner.
Rally Robin (Partners)	Students take turns giving an idea or example orally (Clowes, 2011).
	For example, when using see-think-wonder, each partner takes a turn sharing something they *see* in the photograph, then something they *think* about the photograph. Finally, they take turns sharing something they *wonder* about the photograph.
Whip Around (Groups of three or four)	After posing a question to students, each student shares a response, one at a time, as you "whip around" the table.
	For example, when using see-think-wonder, each student in the group shares something they *see* in the photograph, then something they *think* about the photograph, and finally something they *wonder* about the photograph.

By using cooperative learning, you will ensure that every student has a voice and is actively building the content knowledge and skills they need to eventually answer the compelling question using evidence and reasoning.

Building Your Own Unit

It's time to return to the unit you started building in chapters 1 (page 11) and 2 (page 29) and add the primary source pieces to your four-step planning process template. Figure 3.13 shows an example of step 3 of the four-step planning process for grades K–2.

Figure 3.14 shows an example of step 3 of the four-step planning process for grades 3–5. To learn more about how each source and analysis strategy would look in a daily lesson plan, see Chapter 5 (page 109).

Topic or Unit:	Veterans Day

Step 1: Making Meaning of Standards

Standard: D2.His.3.K-2. GENERATE questions about <u>individuals and groups</u> who have shaped a <u>significant historical change</u>.

Enduring Understanding: Soldiers make sacrifices because they want to protect their country and its citizens.

Compelling Question: What is a hero?

Step 2: Creating Assessments

Classroom-Based Assessment: Whole-class discussion leads to drawing a claim; students might draw a picture of a soldier and label it with the term *hero*.

Doing Social Studies: Students will take informed action by writing thank-you letters to local veterans.

Step 3: Choosing and Analyzing Primary Sources

Primary Source and Close Reading Strategy:

- Photograph: Veterans Day Ceremony at the Vietnam Veterans Memorial www.docsteach.org/documents/document/veterans-day-ceremony-memorial
    - Close Reading Strategy: Hide-and-Seek
- Photograph: Soldiers Carry a Wounded Comrade Through a Swamp www.docsteach.org/documents/document/soldiers-carry-wounded
    - Close Reading Strategy: Visual Thinking
- Photograph: American Reinforcements Arriving on the French Coast www.docsteach.org/documents/document/dday-american-reinforcements
    - Close Reading Strategy: Visual Thinking

Source for standard: NCSS, 2013.

Figure 3.13: Step 3 of the four-step planning process example for grades K–2.

Topic or Unit:	Veterans Day

Step 1: Making Meaning of Standards

Standard: D2.His.6.3-5. DESCRIBE how people's <u>perspectives</u> shaped the <u>historical sources</u> they created.

Enduring Understanding: Our beliefs and values affect our actions.

Compelling Question: How do people's perspectives influence their decisions?

Figure 3.14: Step 3 of the four-step planning process example for grades 3–5.

continued ▶

Step 2: Creating Assessments

Classroom-Based Assessment: Students will answer the compelling question using the claims-evidence-reasoning framework in a written paragraph.

Doing Social Studies: Students will take informed action by writing thank-you letters to local veterans.

Step 3: Choosing and Analyzing Primary Sources

Primary Source and Close Reading Strategy:

- Photograph: Visitors Search for Names on the Vietnam Veterans Memorial
  www.docsteach.org/documents/document/search-names-vietnam-memorial
    - Close Reading Strategy: Jumping In
- Interview: Maya Lin, "Vietnam Veterans Memorial, 1982"
  www.mayalinstudio.com/memory-works/vietnam-veterans-memorial
    - Close Reading Strategy: Ranking
- Letter: "Condolence Letter From President Kennedy to the McAndrews"
  www.docsteach.org/documents/document/kennedy-condolence-mcandrew
    - Close Reading Strategy: Word-Phrase-Sentence

Source for standard: NCSS, 2013.

Continue building your own social studies unit using the template you started in chapters 1 and 2. At this point, complete only step 3, choosing primary sources and the specific close reading strategy you will use when analyzing each primary source.

Summary

In the previous chapters, you learned how to complete the first two steps of the unit planning process: (1) Making Meaning of Social Studies Standards and (2) Creating Assessments. In this chapter, you learned how to complete step 3 of the unit planning process: Choosing and Analyzing Primary Sources. You learned what a primary source is and the importance of using them in your social studies units. You also learned where to find primary sources if they aren't provided with your curriculum resources, or if you are seeking more to use with your units. Next, you learned four historical thinking skills for analyzing primary sources you can use with students as they extract important information from sources needed to make evidence-based claims: sourcing, contextualizing, close reading, and corroborating. Within that process, teacher supports were provided in the form of think-alouds, questions to ask, and strategies and activities to use with students. Additional suggestions were given to increase engagement and participation, including ideas for presenting sources and strategies for student collaboration. In the next chapter, you will learn how to find and use secondary sources.

CHAPTER 4

Step 4: Choosing and Analyzing Secondary Sources

You are now feeling comfortable with finding, choosing, and engaging students with the ideas and content of primary sources, but another issue has arisen. Primary sources alone can't provide all the vocabulary and content knowledge students will need to master the standard you've chosen and answer the compelling question. To ensure that students have all the background knowledge, vocabulary, content, and diverse perspectives needed to answer the compelling question, you will need to use another type of historical source, called a secondary source, in addition to primary sources.

In this chapter, we will look at step 4 of the four-step planning process: Choosing and Analyzing Secondary Sources. We will explore what a secondary source is and the importance of using them in the elementary classroom, along with a list of online places to find elementary-appropriate secondary sources. We will then look at analysis strategies to use before, during, and after reading secondary sources. At the end of the chapter, you will find examples of step 4 of the four-step planning process for grades K–2 and grades 3–5, and then continue creating your own unit by adding secondary sources and analysis strategies to the four-step planning process template you started in chapter 1 (page 11).

Secondary Sources

As stated in chapter 3, "Step 3: Choosing and Analyzing Primary Sources" (page 47), there are two types of historical sources: (1) primary and (2) secondary. As a reminder, the Library of Congress (n.d.b) defines primary sources as "the raw materials of history—original documents and objects that were created at the time under study." These are different from secondary sources, which are defined as "accounts that retell, analyze, or interpret events, usually at a distance of time or place" (Library of Congress, n.d.b). Secondary sources, then, provide an overview of a historical event, figure, or period based on someone's interpretation of the primary sources they studied. For these reasons, it is important to use secondary sources, like textbooks or websites, that are written by trustworthy experts like historians and archivists.

Secondary sources have the same purposes as primary sources: "to spark curiosity, to build knowledge, and to support the development of an argument" (Swan et al., 2018, p. 78). Again, some sources will be used at the beginning of your unit as a hook, others will be used to build knowledge about the content, and others provide the evidence needed to answer the compelling question. For example, you might read the picture book *Veterans: Heroes in Our Neighborhood* (Pfundstein, 2012) to hook your students into a unit about Veterans Day, build their knowledge about the definition of a veteran, or provide evidence that citizens honor veterans because of their sacrifices as your students answer the compelling question, What is a hero? Secondary sources can also enhance students' understanding of primary sources. According to Bober (2019), "A secondary source may help a student understand the confusing elements of a primary source or that a primary source can add depth to the understanding a student gains from a secondary source" (p. 6). For these reasons, it is important to use both primary and secondary sources when planning your units.

Where to Find Secondary Sources

There are several different kinds of secondary sources to use with your social studies units, including textbooks, historically based picture and trade books, and informational articles. Let's take a closer look at each type of secondary source and why you might use it in your social studies unit.

Textbooks

A common secondary source is a district-adopted textbook. Textbooks are useful for building a foundation of knowledge around a topic or event. A textbook's purpose is to summarize knowledge. It is a resource used to support the development of content knowledge along with primary sources (Flygare et al., 2022). But textbooks also have limitations. Professor of literacy education Jennifer L. Altieri (2016) notes that textbooks can be boring or challenging to read, and they often don't offer depth of topics. For these reasons, you want to ensure that you are using a variety of secondary sources and not just a textbook.

Historically Based Picture and Trade Books

Picture books are a great secondary source because students of all ages enjoy listening to their teachers read aloud, and using children's literature is naturally engaging to elementary students. According to Waring (2023), "Literature often offers detailed accounts, complex characters and engaging passages, allowing elementary students to compose understandings in powerful ways" (p. 297). Picture books can support and enhance content-area learning by exposing students to vocabulary and concepts they can't experience firsthand (Wright, 2021). According to Waring (2023), writing for the NCSS:

> Through using children's literature, students can be immersed into someone else's story, or history, and possibly experience some of the emotions the characters display in the literature. The students have an opportunity to reflect on the literature and then corroborate (another historical thinking skill) the stories through use of primary sources and secondary sources. Additionally, by providing students with children's literature on the subject area, the lower-level complex wording, as well as the illustrations, will assist in clearing confusions and misconceptions students may have. (p. 289)

According to classroom teacher and curriculum writer Sarah A. Honore (2022), purposes for using picture books in social studies include:

- Introducing a new topic
- Including a wider range of voices and perspectives on a historical event
- Providing an entry point to a complex topic or a challenging skill
- Supporting a study of primary source documents

There are many lists of picture books related to social studies concepts and topics that teachers can use, but your school library is a good starting place. Your school librarian would love to help you find books related to the topics you are teaching. Another resource is the Notable Social Studies Trade Books for Young People list published each year by NCSS (see www.socialstudies.org/notable-trade-books). You can search for books based on topics or by grade band. When using any text, make sure you read the book beforehand to ensure that the content, perspectives, and issues are appropriate for your students.

It is important to note that according to Waring (2023):

> Picture books are a great way to introduce historical topics to students. But picture books alone will not tell the full and complete story . . . teachers must pair these texts with primary sources to help students learn, see, and understand. (p. 361)

Using the strategies for analyzing primary sources from chapter 3 (page 47), you might pair picture books with primary sources in several different ways.

- Analyze the primary sources *before* reading the picture book to generate questions that can be answered with details in the picture book.

- Analyze the primary sources *before* reading the picture book, and then compare information found in the primary sources to that in the picture book.

- Analyze the primary sources *after* reading the picture book to check the accuracy of the text and images within the picture book against the details in the primary sources.

- Analyze the primary sources *after* reading the picture book to generate wonderings that students still have, which will guide further research.

Another fun way to use picture books is a strategy called book in a day. This strategy aims to engage students in reading a text while also practicing the ELA skills of inferencing and predicting, as well as the social studies skill of contextualizing. To use the strategy, give each student one page from the book. Students read their page and record questions they have about what may have happened before or after their page, questions about the characters, or questions about the events or time period. Then, students pair up and repeat the questioning process with their two pages combined. Next, the partners pair and repeat the questioning process again in their new group of four. Finally, students work together as a whole class to put the pages in order based on their understanding so far, and then read their pages in order as a class. Next, read the book to the students so they can check their thinking. A discussion can follow based on the social studies content or vocabulary your unit focuses on. For example, after using the book in a day strategy with the picture book *This Is Not My Hat* (Klassen, 2012), you can focus on the economic ideas of scarcity, choices, and costs and benefits. In this book, a little fish steals a hat from a big fish. You can focus on the fact that the little fish steals the hat because there are not enough hats (scarcity) and that he made a decision based on the costs and benefits of that choice.

After reading the picture book, you might have students analyze a collection of primary sources related to the book's events or concepts. Lead a conversation about whether the book matches the evidence from the primary sources. This is the historical thinking skill of corroboration.

To use this strategy with lower elementary grade students, you may need to provide the beginning and ending pages and have them try to fill in a few pages in the middle of the book. You could also provide small groups with pages from the beginning, middle, or end of the book. That way students are not trying to put the entire book in order but rather they are focused on ordering only a few pages at a time.

For upper elementary grade students, you can use the strategy with chapter books. Give each pair of students a chapter from a book and have them write a summary of that chapter. Then, pairs stand in order of their chapters and read their summaries. At the end, students will have read an entire chapter book in a day! The *Who Was?* book series (www.whowasbookseries.com/who-was) works great for this activity because reading the chapters out of order won't affect the overall understanding of the text.

Integration Idea
ELA

When integrating literature, like picture books, into your social studies lessons, it is important to remember to keep the social studies skills and processes the focal point of your lessons. Using a book about a social studies topic in your ELA instruction is not the same as teaching effective, enduring social studies concepts. Social studies educators Andrea S. Libresco and Jeannette Balantic (2013) offer the following ideas for effective integration of ELA and social studies with picture books:

- Create a sociogram of the characters in the book.
- Make a timeline of the events in the story.
- Sketch a map of the story's setting.
- Generate a list of questions sparked by events or characters' choices in the book.
- Re-write parts of the book from different characters' points of view.
- Craft different endings for the book to explore what is either possible or desirable. (p. 4)

Informational Articles

If your district does not have a district-adopted curriculum that provides a textbook or text-based resources, there are many online resources available that provide a range of grade-level-appropriate informational articles. Table 4.1 provides a summary of online resources available for finding secondary sources, including picture books and articles.

Table 4.1: Online Resources for Finding Secondary Sources

Online Resource	Types of Content
Notable Social Studies Trade Books (www.socialstudies.org/notable-trade-books)	• Trade books (picture and chapter)
Knowledge Quest Blogs by Tom Bober (https://knowledgequest.aasl.org/author/tbober)	• Pairing primary sources with picture books
Database of Award-Winning Children's Literature (http://dawcl.com)	• Trade books (picture and chapter)
NewsELA (https://newsela.com)	• Articles
ReadWorks (www.readworks.org)	• Articles
TextProject (https://textproject.org)	• Picture books, articles
Achieve the Core (https://achievethecore.org/category/411/ela-literacy-lessons?filter_cat=1254&sort=date)	• Articles
CommonLit (www.commonlit.org)	• Articles
Britannica Kids (https://kids.britannica.com)	• Articles (encyclopedia entries)

Secondary Source Analysis Strategies

Students will need analysis strategies so that they can comprehend the secondary sources and make connections to the unit's big ideas. The goal of these strategies is to guide students to think like historians or social studies experts as they read secondary sources, such as articles, textbooks, or picture books.

Because you are choosing content-rich, complex texts, you need to think about what strategies your students will need to access those texts. All the strategies in this section can be used with secondary sources. These strategies are organized by *before-reading* strategies to prepare students to engage with the text, *during-reading* strategies to support students as they extract the information they will need for understanding the content, and *after-reading* strategies as they reflect on and synthesize their new learning.

While there are many literacy goals when working with texts, this book focuses on reading social studies texts with the purpose of gaining evidence to answer the compelling question. Ask yourself the following question when choosing strategies to use before, during, and after reading: "What are the main ideas I want students to walk away with after reading the text?" Your answer will guide your decision making. If there are vocabulary words important to the main idea, choose a vocabulary strategy before reading. During reading, make the main idea the focus of the annotating. After reading, make the main idea the focus of student writing or discussion. For example, imagine you are reading a picture book about veterans during a unit on Veterans Day. The main ideas you want students to walk away with are the definition of a veteran and how people honor veterans. Before reading, you might choose to have students create a Frayer Model of the word *veteran*. During reading, you might ask students to listen for the different ways veterans are celebrated. Then after reading, you might use a discussion strategy as students share their thoughts about how people honor veterans. The important thing is to purposefully choose strategies based on the content and enduring understandings you want students to learn.

The before-, during-, and after-reading strategies in this chapter aren't the only ones you can use with secondary sources—they're simply those that I have found work well with social studies informational texts. Feel free to use strategies you and your students are already comfortable with as you work with secondary sources. It is also important to remember the purpose of secondary sources in the elementary classroom—to build knowledge and gain evidence to answer the compelling question. You can create an anchor chart with the compelling question on it and record the sources and evidence you find to answer the compelling question throughout your unit. This ensures that you bring each source, primary or secondary, back to the goal of the unit.

Before-Reading Strategies

First, we will consider strategies to use before reading, sometimes referred to as *prereading strategies*. Argentar and colleagues (2021) offer the "four Ps of social studies prereading" (p. 48). These prereading strategies can be used with any secondary source when introducing it to students. Argentar and colleagues (2021) suggest that teachers should "focus on one or two prereading strategies with students" (p. 49). You should purposefully think about which of these prereading strategies will be most important for your students to ensure comprehension of the content. For example, if the text structure is unfamiliar to your students, you may want to focus on previewing the text. These prereading strategies are explained in table 4.2.

Table 4.2: The Four Ps of Social Studies Prereading

P of Prereading	Explanation
Preview	The student will scan the text to review subheadings and text features.
Predict	The student will think about what they might learn based on their preview.
Prior Knowledge	The student will think about what they already know about the topic.
Purpose	The student will think about the teacher-provided reason for reading the text and why the author wrote the text.

Source: Argentar et al., 2021.

Strategies for Building Vocabulary Knowledge

Secondary sources in social studies are often full of new vocabulary. It is important to build students' understanding of these words before they begin reading the text. It is also important to establish a purpose for reading the source. When students know why they are reading a text, it can lead to greater comprehension. The following sections provide strategies for building vocabulary knowledge and establishing a purpose for reading when using secondary sources.

Frayer Model

A Frayer Model is a graphic organizer to help students understand complex vocabulary (Argentar et al., 2021). This strategy deepens students' understanding of a word they are already familiar with (Hennessy, 2021). Students place the vocabulary word in the center of the model and then complete each of the following activities in the four quadrants surrounding the word: define the word, list characteristics of the word, provide examples or pictures of the word, and provide nonexamples of the word. When choosing vocabulary related to social studies, focus on words that can have more than one meaning or words that are critical to understanding the content or big idea. For example, when students hear the word *market*, they may think of a grocery store or farmers' market, but in economics, the word *market* can also refer to a type of economic system in which "economic decisions and the pricing of goods and services are guided by the interactions of a country's individual citizens and businesses" (Investopedia Team, 2024). Figure 4.1 shows a completed Frayer Model for the word *veteran*. Please see appendix A (page 127) for a blank template.

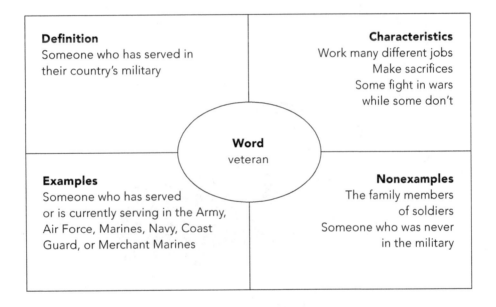

Figure 4.1: Completed Frayer Model for the word *veteran*.

Linking Language

This strategy involves making predictions about the meanings of vocabulary words based on images, so it works best with words students are unfamiliar with. The first step is to choose four or five words from a text that are unknown to your students but are critical for them to understand to make meaning of the text. Next, find images that represent the words. Attach each of the images to a large sheet of paper and post the sheets around the room. The paper should contain only the image at this point. Then, students move in groups of four or five from image to image and record on the sheets words they associate with the featured images. They should focus on their senses—what they see, think, and feel while studying the images. After all the groups have rotated through all the images, they return to the original poster they started with. Students connect related words using lines and circles. Teams work together to guess which word matches their image. Then the teacher reveals the words that the images represent along with their definitions. After reading the text, students can use sticky notes to add additional words with the new understanding they've gained from the text. Students then use the words in a writing piece to continue practicing. For lower elementary grade students, this may be a few sentences about the text, and for upper elementary grade students, this may be a paragraph summarizing what they learned or answering a question about the text. Figure 4.2 is an example of a linking language poster for the word *tyranny*.

Figure 4.2: Linking language poster for the word *tyranny*.

Vocabulary Knowledge Rating

When we really understand a word's meaning, we can give an informal explanation of the word, identify synonyms and antonyms, provide categorical information, and describe concepts that the word represents (Wright, 2021). For these reasons, it can be helpful to think of word-meaning knowledge as a continuum. Having students rate their knowledge of a word before reading signals them to look for and try to deepen their understanding of that word while reading—to move along the knowledge continuum. Writing for ReadingRockets.org, authors Katherine A. Dougherty Stahl and Marco A. Bravo (2010) explain that:

> Vocabulary knowledge is multifaceted. Word knowledge is acquired incrementally. At each stage or point on a continuum of word knowledge, students might be familiar with the term, know words related to the term, or have flexibility with using it in both written and oral form. It is clear that to know a word is more than to know its definition.

You can use a vocabulary knowledge rating scale to assess prior understanding and to assist students with self-assessment and setting goals. Provide students with a list of words from the text and ask them to rate their understanding of the words on a scale. After reading, return to the scale to have students rate their knowledge of the words once again. Encourage students to use these words in discussions and writing after they finish reading. This will help students continue to deepen their understanding of the vocabulary words. Figure 4.3 (page 92) is a vocabulary knowledge rating scale example for students to use prior to reading the Preamble to the United States Constitution. The grade you teach and the length of the text will help you determine how many words to put in your rating scale. For example, a kindergarten teacher may focus on two words from a text while a fifth-grade teacher using a longer text may use seven words. Please see appendix A (page 127) for a blank reproducible version of this figure.

Word Sorts

Word sorts encourage students to process and reflect on their understanding of new words and how those relate to known words (Wright, 2021). You can provide students with cards that contain vocabulary words from the text before reading. Students should sort the cards into categories based on their understanding of the words before reading about a topic. Students can glue their sorts to a large sheet of paper or take a picture of the completed sort. After reading the text, have students revise their thinking by redoing the sort (if a picture was

Word	I Know It Well 1	I Have Seen or Heard It 2	I Have No Clue 3
union			
justice			
tranquility			
defense			
welfare			
liberty			
posterity			

Source: Adapted from Dougherty Stahl & Bravo, 2010

Figure 4.3: Vocabulary knowledge rating scale example.

taken) or using lines and arrows to show how they would resort the words (if they were glued to a sheet of paper). After they finish sorting their words, students should label the different sorts with category names. Then, students can defend their thinking by discussing connections and conceptual understanding to a partner. For example, when the class is reading about the three branches of the U.S. government, words from the text might include the following: Congress, Supreme Court, President, Cabinet, House of Representatives, and Senate. After reading, students' sorts might include categories like Executive Branch, Legislative Branch, and Judicial Branch. Figures 4.4 and 4.5 show both before-reading and after-reading sorts for this example.

Strategies for Establishing Purpose

Having a clear purpose in mind before reading a source enables students to have a plan as they read, activate background knowledge, and sort important information (Hennessy, 2021). The following strategies will help with these goals as students work with secondary sources.

Anticipation Guides

Anticipation guides not only create a purpose for reading but also allow students to make predictions using prior knowledge. To use this strategy, provide students with a list of statements that are presented as facts prior to reading a text. The statements should be related to important vocabulary, events, or ideas within the text. Using prior knowledge and prediction, students will mark whether they agree with the statement. Students aim to find answers to these statements while reading. After reading, students respond to the statements

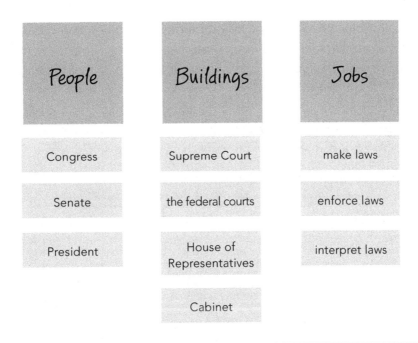

Figure 4.4: Before-reading sort example.

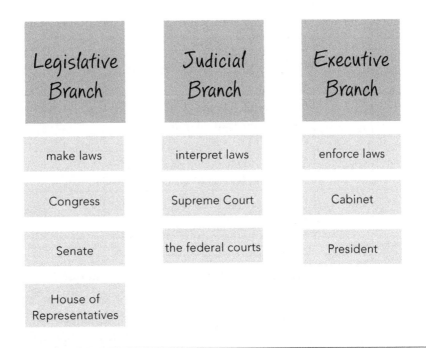

Figure 4.5: After-reading sort example.

again, this time providing evidence from the text to support their thinking. Students can write their evidence or can discuss it in small groups. To adapt this strategy for lower elementary grade students, you can read the statements to them, and they can mark agree or disagree, or you can have everyone indicate a response with a thumbs-up or thumbs-down and then record the class's collective answer on a chart. Figure 4.6 is an example of an anticipation guide for a fifth-grade text about the causes of the American Revolution.

Anticipation Guide: Causes of the American Revolution					
Before Reading				After Reading	
Agree	Disagree			Agree	Disagree
		The French and Indian War was fought between the French and the Native Americans.			
		The Proclamation of 1763 was a public announcement made by King George stating that all land west of the Appalachian Mountains belonged to the Native Americans.			
		When King George and Parliament passed the Stamp Act and the Quartering Act, colonists reacted by protesting.			
		If you participate in a boycott, you refuse to buy certain goods or services.			
		Both colonists and British soldiers died at the Boston Massacre.			
		The Boston Tea Party was a peaceful meeting between colonists and members of the British Parliament.			

Figure 4.6: Anticipation guide for a fifth-grade text about the American Revolution.

Subheadings Into Questions

This strategy enables students to set a purpose for reading, as well as predict what the text will be about. Before reading, students read the subheadings and turn each one into a question. During reading, students look for the answers to their questions. For example, a subheading about the Boston Tea Party might be *A Serious Tea Party*. Students might turn this into the question, Why was the tea party serious? After reading, students return to their questions to see whether they can answer them.

Picture Books

Sometimes the secondary source text that you want students to read requires prerequisite knowledge of ideas, events, time periods, or individuals. It can be helpful to build background knowledge around these topics by using picture books. Then, students can make connections to the information in the picture book while reading the secondary source, or, if appropriate, they may even find discrepancies between the information in the picture book and the secondary source. This can be used as a springboard for further research or corroboration with primary sources. For example, during a unit about civic rights and responsibilities, you might want to read a secondary source about the civic responsibility of voting. The source might reference various suffragists and the suffragist movement without explaining who or what this is. To build understanding of this topic, you might choose to read the picture book *Equality's Call: The Story of Voting Rights in America* (Diesen, 2020). This book explains the history of voting rights for various groups and how not everyone had the right to vote for a long time. Now that students understand the history of voting rights, they will better understand the secondary source about voting.

During-Reading Strategies

Before-reading strategies prepare students for reading secondary sources through building vocabulary knowledge and establishing a purpose, but students still need additional strategies to help them find meaning within the text *while* they read. According to Argentar and colleagues (2021), students change from "passive participants into active thinkers" as they begin to read the text (p. 86). This means that students shouldn't just read the words on the page— they need to begin to make meaning and gain new understanding as they read the text. Each of the following strategies helps students think about what they are reading to aid understanding.

Text Chunking

Informational text, often written in unfamiliar language and structures, can be overwhelming for students. According to Argentar and colleagues (2021), chunking text "allows students to break the text into manageable parts, giving

Integration Idea
ELA

When writing historically based picture books, many authors and illustrators will use primary sources as they research and illustrate the topic, event, or historical figure. In addition, many times the authors share their journeys through this research in the backs of their books or in interviews that can be found online. Your students can study this process as they create their own informational writing, using primary sources to guide the writing and illustrating of their own books. In addition, the interviews can be viewed as an oral history, which is a primary source. Students could use a primary source analysis strategy from chapter 3 (page 47) as they analyze the interview's transcript. This is also true for the authors of historically based chapter books. For example, Lauren Tarshis, author of the *I Survived* series, loves to share her research process. Check out www.laurentarshis.com for virtual field trips to several locations discussed in her books.

them chances to take thinking breaks and compartmentalize what they've read" (p. 97). It forces students to slow their thinking and process what they're reading. To chunk the text, you should identify stopping points within the text and questions students should answer at the end of each chunk, either independently on paper or in small discussion groups. As students get older, they can generate their own questions at the end of each chunk.

Annotation

Annotation of secondary sources is similar to how it is used when analyzing text-based primary sources from chapter 3 (page 47). The difference is in how you will use the annotations. With primary sources, you are making observations to inspire questioning or inferring through the use of historical thinking skills. With secondary sources, you are trying to make meaning. Therefore, it is important to return to students' annotations and ensure through small- or whole-group discussion that students' misconceptions or questions are addressed. You can use the same annotations as discussed in chapter 3 (page 47), including highlighting, underlining, writing questions or ideas in the margin, or using symbols while reading the text (Monte-Sano, 2018).

Thinking Jobs

One of the before-reading goals was to establish a purpose for reading. It is important for you to communicate this purpose to the students. Nickelsen and Dickson (2022) suggest using what they call a *thinking job*, which they describe as "a teacher-friendly way to plan for a student-friendly purpose for reading" (p. 98). It might be as simple as saying, "Listen for _____ as I read," or more intensive, such as having students take notes, annotate, or find evidence of a claim as they read. You should communicate the thinking job to students in the form of a question and then an action stem. For example, you might ask students, "What is a veteran?" before reading aloud the picture book *What Is a Veteran, Anyway?* (Snyder, 2016), and then tell students that their thinking job is to listen for different examples of veterans as you read the book. With lower elementary grade students, you might have them raise their hands when they hear an example, and you could record their ideas on a class anchor chart. For upper elementary grade students, you could have them record their ideas on a sheet of paper as you read, then discuss their thinking in pairs or small groups and create a class anchor chart after reading. When using articles, students can underline, circle, or highlight the answers to their thinking job.

Text Structure Graphic Organizers

Writers of informational text often organize the information using different text structures. Five common text structures are (1) sequence, (2) compare and contrast, (3) cause and effect, (4) problem and solution, and (5) description. According to educators Jane Oakhill, Kate Cain, and Carsten Elbro (2015):

> Readers who are familiar with the particular structure of the text have several advantages: they know what to expect from different parts of the text, where to search for particular types of information, and how the different parts of the text are linked together. (p. 82)

Therefore, it is essential to not only explicitly teach text structure but to also help students organize the information based on text structures while they read. Text structure graphic organizers are one way to do this. Graphic organizers enable readers to organize information in a way that lets them see relationships and then identify important information (Hennessy, 2021). Although identified here as a during-reading strategy, text structure graphic organizers can be used before, during, and after reading. For example, before reading, you will want to display and explain the graphic organizer and make connections to students' prior knowledge on the topic. Students can fill in details from the text during reading and then use the organizer for discussion and summarization after reading. A simple Google search for the text structure type offers many free graphic organizers. For example, if you are reading a secondary source about the characteristics of a good citizen, you could tell students that the text features a description structure. Explain to them that the text will give examples and characteristics of a good citizen. During reading, students can fill in a concept map graphic organizer. Figure 4.7 shows an example of a concept map graphic organizer for the word *citizen*.

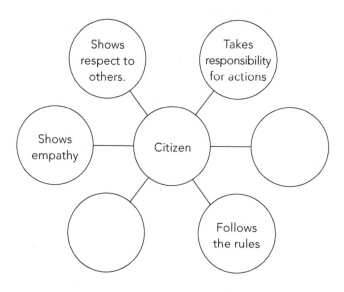

Figure 4.7: Concept map for the word *citizen*.

After-Reading Strategies

Finally, we will look at after-reading strategies. According to AdLit (n.d.), *after-reading strategies* "provide students an opportunity to summarize, question, reflect, discuss, and respond to text." This can be accomplished through individual or small-group writing and discussion opportunities. According to Argentar and colleagues (2021), students need to realize that the thinking doesn't stop after reading a text. It is through thoughtful reflections that students can integrate the learning from primary and secondary sources to create enduring understandings and procure the evidence needed to answer the compelling question.

Writing Strategies

According to education writer Natalie Wexler (2019), writing "can serve as a powerful means of pushing students to review facts they've been taught, make connections, and think about them analytically" (p. 40). Writing about reading has additional purposes; it allows the learner to clarify their thinking (Hennessy, 2021). It also allows students to develop and deepen their understanding of vocabulary when they use those words in their writing. Writing after reading a secondary source could be as simple as a one- or two-sentence summary of the text for upper elementary grade students or a drawing with a caption of a main idea for lower elementary grade students. Always encourage students to use the vocabulary from your before-reading activities in their writing, since students need at least fifteen to twenty exposures to new words before they can understand them enough to apply their meaning (Hennessy, 2021). Here are additional strategies to use when you want your students to write about their reading.

Five Words

This strategy from Argentar and colleagues (2021) asks students to "evaluate all the information in the text and prioritize what is most critical to understanding" (p. 113). After reading, students individually underline, highlight, or circle the five most important words in the text. Next, students share their words in small groups and provide reasons behind why they chose those five words as the most important. Finally, each group comes to a consensus on the five most important words from the text and shares their five words with the whole class. Teachers can use this discussion to help students summarize the text and then think about what information from the text provides evidence to answer the compelling question.

3-2-1 Exit Ticket

This strategy from Argentar and colleagues (2021) gives students the opportunity to synthesize their learning while simultaneously providing feedback to the teacher on depth of understanding. Students write down three key terms, two key details, and one important person or event from the text (Argentar et al., 2021). Younger students can use drawings to represent the answers to the 3-2-1 reflection, or the teacher can lead a whole-group discussion about the questions. You can use this as a formative assessment or as a form of individual reflection before students participate in discussions.

Writing Questions

This strategy provides a way to find and summarize the text's main ideas. Divide students into groups of three or four after they have read a secondary source in the form of an article or section of a textbook. Assign each person in the group a different chunk of the text. Students then write three questions (with answers) about their assigned text. After all students have written questions, have them use their questions to quiz their group members. Finally, each group chooses their best two questions to share with the whole group.

Consider using question stems based on educational psychologist Benjamin S. Bloom's (1956) taxonomy to ensure that students are going beyond surface-level questions. The questions in table 4.3 come from education authors LeAnn Nickelsen and Melissa Dickson's (2019) book *Teaching With the Instructional Cha-Chas*. They suggest putting question stems on stars and requiring students to write a question using the stems from each level of stars (Nickelsen & Dickson, 2019).

Table 4.3: Question Stems for Question Stars

Question Level	Question Stems
1. Knowledge	Who or what is _____? How would you explain _____? Can you list three _____?
2. Comprehension	How would you compare or contrast _____ and _____? Which statements support _____? How would you summarize _____?
3. Application	What will result if _____? What examples can you find for _____? How will you solve _____?
4. Analysis	How is _____ related to _____? What conclusion can you draw about _____? What evidence supports _____?
5. Evaluation	How will you prove or disprove _____? Why is it better that _____? What will you cite to defend the actions of _____?

Source: Adapted from Bloom, 1956; Nickelsen & Dickson, 2019.

Discussion Strategies

Discussion allows students to share and continue developing the enduring understandings that are a main component of social studies instruction. According to Waring (2023), "During discussions, teachers (a) help students establish ground rules for interacting, (b) initiate the conversation by asking thought-provoking questions, (c) monitor students' interaction, and (d) assess students' participation and learning about the topic being discussed" (p. 37).

The following sections provide discussion strategies you can use with students after they have read secondary sources. Before using these strategies, you will want to explicitly teach your students how to participate in an effective discussion using talk moves. *Talk moves* are sentence starters that students use to join a discussion, whether whole group or small group (Edutopia, 2018). Table 4.4 outlines several different talk moves and sentence frames for students to use as they engage in each talk move. These can be modeled and used one at a time to strengthen group conversations. For lower elementary grade students, you may choose to focus on only a few talk moves at a time.

Table 4.4: Talk Moves for Discussion

Talk Move	Sentence Frame
Add On	"I would like to add on to what _____ said."
Reason	"I agree [or disagree] because _____."
Repeat	"I heard you say _____."
Revoice	"What I think you said was _____."
Request More	"Can you say more about _____?"
Press for Reasoning	"What is your evidence for _____?"

Source: Edutopia, 2018.

Hexagonal Thinking

According to educator Betsy Potash (2020), hexagonal thinking is a discussion strategy that engages participants in a conversation about making connections among ideas and concepts. A hexagon has six sides, which provides six different ways each one can connect to another hexagon, which is the main purpose of this strategy. The teacher writes words (vocabulary, people, events, or ideas) from the text on small paper hexagons (teachers could use images for lower elementary grade students). Each student in a small group takes a turn connecting one hexagon to another while explaining how it connects to the other hexagons it is touching. For example, a student could connect a hexagon that reads *the Boston Tea Party* to one that reads *the Intolerable Acts* because the first event was a cause of the second event. Or lower elementary grade students might connect a hexagon with a picture of a child throwing away their trash to a hexagon that says *being responsible* after reading about the characteristics of a good citizen. If you want to add a written component, students can write about several of the connections in their hexagonal thinking organizer. Another tip is to give groups several blank hexagons and have them decide on more words or phrases to add. Students can then individually write about how this word connects to the other words. Googling *hexagonal thinking* will bring up fillable hexagon templates that you can print and use. Figure 4.8 provides an example of a hexagonal thinking activity over a text about the Bill of Rights.

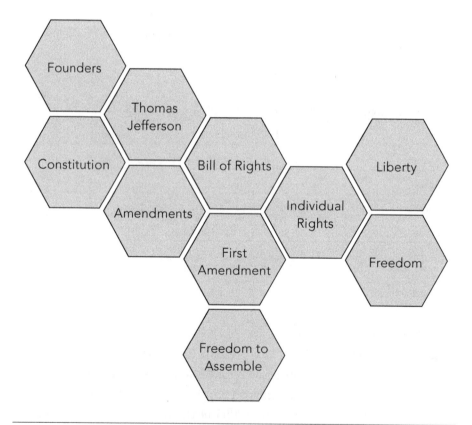

Figure 4.8: Hexagonal thinking activity example.

Hot Seat

This interactive strategy enables students to become experts on an aspect of a text (for example, a topic, event, or historical figure) and then respond to questions from their small-group members based on their knowledge from the text. After reading a text, divide students into groups of four. To use this strategy, one person in each group starts in the hot seat. Two members of the group will ask that person questions about information in the text while the fourth member of the group becomes the lifeline for the person in the hot seat, in case they need support in answering their questions. Each person in the group takes a turn being in the hot seat, being a lifeline, and asking questions. This strategy allows groups to make connections, review content, and discuss enduring understandings. If this is the first time you are using this strategy, you may need to provide questions or question stems for students to ask the person in the hot seat. Students can generate their own questions if you have used this strategy before.

Inside-Outside Circle

This strategy allows all students to practice speaking and listening with teacher-generated questions to review content, make connections, or discuss enduring understandings. In this strategy, half of the class makes a circle in the middle of the room by standing shoulder to shoulder and facing the outside of the circle. Then, the other half of the class comes and stands in front of them so that each person is facing a partner. The teacher then provides a question and identifies who will speak first: the partner on the inside or the outside of the circle. After discussing the question, the teacher directs either the inside or the outside circle to rotate. Students might rotate two places to their left or maybe three places to their right, but the goal is to have each student discuss with another random partner. They can discuss the same question again to hear a different perspective, or the teacher might provide a new question or prompt. Another option is that the teacher might ask each person to share what their previous partner said before sharing their own thoughts. This allows students to practice listening skills and hear multiple perspectives about the topic.

When choosing before-, during-, or after-reading strategies with secondary sources, it is important to remember that the goal of using these sources in your social studies classroom is to build knowledge and gain evidence to answer the compelling question. This will lead to purposeful decision making when choosing which strategies to use.

Integration Idea
ELA and Mathematics

In their book *Civil Discourse: Classroom Conversations for Stronger Communities*, Joe Schmidt and Nichelle Pinkney (2022) identify three types of discourse: (1) dialogue, (2) discussion, and (3) debate. "Dialogue," explain authors Bruce Wellman and Laura Lipton (2017), "promotes a spirit of inquiry within a group. The purpose is to generate multiple perspectives, encourage connection making between ideas and people, and develop shared understandings" (p. 40). Discussion is "more than a sharing of ideas," as opposing views are presented and defended (Schmidt & Pinkney, 2022, p. 50). Often a team consensus is the goal. "Debate is an extreme form of discussion, in which the format dictates that people take sides and advocate for that side" (Easton, 2015).

All three types of discourse should be used in social studies. For example, when students are analyzing primary sources, the discourse they are involved in is most likely dialogue. The goal is to make connections and identify perspectives. There is a shared outcome. Discussion would be a preferred type of discourse when students are answering compelling questions and providing evidence and reasoning to defend their point of view or thoughts about that question. Finally, debate might be used when teaching students how to make claims and support them with evidence. But the skill of discourse can be practiced and refined in other parts of your day with other content areas. For example, students are engaged in dialogue when they generate multiple perspectives about the theme of a story, they are engaged in discussion when they are trying to reach consensus about which activity they will choose as a class reward, and they are engaged in debate when they take a side regarding which mathematics strategy would be the most efficient when solving word problems. In the introduction (page 1), we established that one of the reasons we need social studies in the elementary classroom is to prepare students for their civic responsibilities. Learning how to participate in civil discourse will serve them well for this role in a democracy.

Building Your Own Unit

It's time to return to the unit you started building in chapters 1 (page 11) through 3 (page 47) and add the secondary source pieces to your four-step planning process template. Figure 4.9 shows an example of step 4 of the four-step planning process for grades K–2.

Topic or Unit:	Veterans Day

Step 1: Making Meaning of Standards

Standard: D2.His.3.K-2. GENERATE questions about <u>individuals and groups</u> who have shaped a <u>significant historical change</u>.

Enduring Understanding: Soldiers make sacrifices because they want to protect their country and its citizens.

Compelling Question: What is a hero?

Step 2: Creating Assessments

Classroom-Based Assessment: Whole-class discussion leads to drawing a claim; students might draw a picture of a soldier and label it with the term *hero*.

Doing Social Studies: Students will take informed action by writing thank-you letters to local veterans.

Step 3: Choosing and Analyzing Primary Sources

Primary Source and Close Reading Strategy:

- Photograph: Veterans Day Ceremony at the Vietnam Veterans Memorial www.docsteach.org/documents/document/veterans-day-ceremony-memorial
  - Close Reading Strategy: Hide-and-Seek
- Photograph: Soldiers Carry a Wounded Comrade Through a Swamp www.docsteach.org/documents/document/soldiers-carry-wounded
  - Close Reading Strategy: Visual Thinking
- Photograph: American Reinforcements Arriving on the French Coast www.docsteach.org/documents/document/dday-american-reinforcements
  - Close Reading Strategy: Visual Thinking

Figure 4.9: Step 4 of the four-step planning process example for grades K–2.

continued ▶

Step 4: Choosing and Analyzing Secondary Sources

Secondary Source and Before-, During-, and After-Reading Strategies:

- Picture Book: *Veterans: Heroes in Our Neighborhood* by Valerie Pfundstein (2012)
  - Before: Frayer Model for the word *veteran*
  - During: Text structure graphic organizer—description
  - After: Five words
- Picture Book: *The Wall* by Eve Bunting (2001)
  - Before: Anticipation guide
  - During: Chunking the text
  - After: Hot seat
- Picture Book: *Proud as a Peacock, Brave as a Lion* by Jane Barclay (2009)
  - Before: Frayer Model for the word *monument*
  - During: Chunking the text
  - After: Hot seat

Source for standard: NCSS, 2013.

Figure 4.10 shows an example of step 4 of the four-step planning process for grades 3–5. To learn more about how each source and analysis strategy would look in a daily lesson plan, see Chapter 5 (page 109).

Use the unit you began planning in chapters 1–3 to continue building your own social studies unit. If you would like to transfer everything to a clean template, return to the reproducible "The Four-Step Planning Process Template" (page 128) in appendix A. At this point, complete only step 4, choosing secondary sources, as well as the specific before-, during-, and after-reading strategies you will use with each source.

Topic or Unit:	Veterans Day
Step 1: Making Meaning of Standards	

Standard: D2.His.6.3-5. DESCRIBE how people's <u>perspectives</u> shaped the <u>historical sources</u> they created.

Enduring Understanding: Our beliefs and values affect our actions.

Compelling Question: How do people's perspectives influence their decisions?

Step 2: Creating Assessments

Classroom-Based Assessment: Students will answer the compelling question using the claims-evidence-reasoning framework in a written paragraph.

Doing Social Studies: Students will take informed action by writing thank-you letters to local veterans.

Step 3: Choosing and Analyzing Primary Sources

Primary Source and Close Reading Strategy:

- Photograph: Visitors Search for Names on the Vietnam Veterans Memorial www.docsteach.org/documents/document/search-names-vietnam-memorial
  - Close Reading Strategy: Jumping In
- Interview: Maya Lin, "Vietnam Veterans Memorial, 1982" www.mayalinstudio.com/memory-works/vietnam-veterans-memorial
  - Close Reading Strategy: Ranking
- Letter: "Condolence Letter From President Kennedy to the McAndrews" www.docsteach.org/documents/document/kennedy-condolence-mcandrew
  - Close Reading Strategy: Word-Phrase-Sentence

Step 4: Choosing and Analyzing Secondary Sources

Secondary Source and Before-, During-, and After-Reading Strategies:

- Picture Book: *Maya Lin: Artist-Architect of Light and Lines* by Jeanne Walker Harvey (2017)
  - Before: Frayer Model for the word *memorial*
  - During: Chunking the text
  - After: Hot seat
- Informational Article: "Vietnam War" www.history.com/topics/vietnam-war/vietnam-war-history
  - Before: Anticipation guide
  - During: Text structure graphic organizer—description
  - After: Five words
- Picture Book: *The Wall* by Eve Bunting (2001)
  - Before: Anticipation guide
  - During: Text structure graphic organizer—cause and effect
  - After: Hot seat

Source for standard: NCSS, 2013.

Figure 4.10: Step 4 of the four-step planning process example for grades 3–5.

Summary

In the previous chapters, you learned how to complete the first three steps of the unit planning process: (1) Making Meaning of Social Studies Standards, (2) Creating Assessments, and (3) Choosing and Analyzing Primary Sources. In this chapter, you learned how to complete the fourth and final step of the unit planning process: Choosing and Analyzing Secondary Sources. You learned what secondary sources are and the importance of using them in your social studies units. You also learned where to find secondary sources if they aren't provided with your curriculum resources or if you are seeking more to use with your units. Then, you learned before-, during-, and after-reading strategies for analyzing secondary sources that you can use with students to help them understand and gain information from the sources needed to make evidence-based claims. In the next chapter, you will learn how to take your completed templates and turn them into daily lesson plans.

CHAPTER 5

Turning Your Unit Into Daily Lesson Plans

At this point, you have curated a collection of primary and secondary sources that will help your students build topic knowledge, as well as provide evidence to support a claim while answering your unit's compelling question. But how do you take this broad planning template and turn it into daily lessons? In this chapter, we will explore how to take your completed unit planning template and use it to guide your daily lesson plans. Then, we will review answers to questions teachers may have during the implementation process.

Building Daily Lessons

The first step in using your planning template is to think about the order in which you will use your sources. The goal is to arrange the sources in a sequence that will enable students to build knowledge and gain evidence to answer the unit's compelling question. In chapter 3 (page 47), we created a chart that listed the content and ideas we wanted students to learn in the unit and then matched those to primary and secondary sources (figure 3.2, page 54). We will need to create another chart that is more specific regarding the content or ideas from each source, as well as add another component: identifying the exact sequence in which we will use the sources. As a reminder, chapter 3 states that sources have three purposes: "to spark curiosity, to build knowledge, and to support the development of an argument" (Swan et al., 2018, p. 78).

For each of your sources, you will need to decide which purposes it fulfills, which will guide where it should be placed in the unit sequence. Begin by identifying all the sources, determining each source's purpose, and then numbering the sources based on the order in which you will use them. Figure 5.1 (page 111) is a chart that shows this process of taking sources and intentionally sequencing them toward answering the unit's compelling question in a Veterans Day unit for grade 2.

The next step is to think about how you will use each source in your daily lesson plans. Figure 5.2 (page 113) shows how a second-grade teacher could use the plans from the completed K–2 planning template example (see figure 4.9, page 105) and the planned sequencing of sources for that example (see figure 5.1) to create daily lesson plans in a social studies or reading block over the course of five days.

Figure 5.3 (page 117) is a chart that shows the process of taking sources and intentionally sequencing them toward answering the unit's compelling question in a Veterans Day unit for grade 5.

Figure 5.4 (page 119) shows how a fifth-grade teacher could use the Veterans Day planning template to create daily lesson plans in a social studies or reading block over the course of six days.

Source	Purpose	Sequence
Photograph: Veterans Day Ceremony at the Vietnam Veterans Memorial (www.docsteach.org/documents/document/veterans-day-ceremony-memorial)	• Sparks curiosity	1
Photograph: Soldiers Carry a Wounded Comrade Through a Swamp (www.docsteach.org/documents/document/soldiers-carry-wounded)	• Builds knowledge about what a soldier does • Provides evidence to support the argument that soldiers are heroic	4
Photograph: American Reinforcements Arriving on the French Coast (www.docsteach.org/documents/document/dday-american-reinforcements)	• Builds knowledge about what a soldier does • Provides evidence to support the argument that soldiers are heroic	4
Picture Book: *Veterans: Heroes in Our Neighborhood* by Valerie Pfundstein (2012)	• Builds knowledge about the definition of *veteran* • Provides evidence to support the argument that veterans are important	2
Picture Book: *The Wall* by Eve Bunting (2001)	• Builds knowledge about the definition of *monument* • Provides evidence to support the argument that monuments honor veterans' sacrifices	3
Picture Book: *Proud as a Peacock, Brave as a Lion* by Jane Barclay (2009)	• Provides evidence to support the argument that veterans are heroic, and we honor them with monuments	5

Figure 5.1: Sequencing sources in a Veterans Day unit for grade 2.

Step Number	Include the task, primary or secondary source and analysis strategy (from the K–2 planning template example shown in figure 4.9, page 105), and purpose (from K–2 example of planned sequencing shown in figure 5.1, page 111)	Plan
		Day 1
1	**Source:** Photograph—Veterans Day Ceremony at the Vietnam Veterans Memorial **Strategy:** Hide-and-seek **Purpose:** Spark curiosity	Give each student a copy of the photograph Veterans Day Ceremony at the Vietnam Veterans Memorial or project the photograph so everyone can see it. Don't tell the students the title of the photograph or provide any background information at this point in the lesson. Analyze the photograph using the hide-and-seek primary source analysis strategy (see chapter 3, page 47) to get students thinking about what they might see, hear, smell, or touch if they were present at this event. Ask students what they think is going on based on their observations after using the analysis strategy.
2	**Task:** Introduce the compelling question, What is a hero?	Introduce the compelling question. Explain to students that the photograph they just analyzed shows people honoring heroes, and that over the next few days, they will learn more about who these people are and what makes them heroes.
3	**Source:** Picture book—*Veterans: Heroes in Our Neighborhood* (Pfundstein, 2012) **Before-Reading Strategy:** Four Ps of social studies prereading **Purpose:** Build knowledge about the definition of *veteran*; provide evidence to support the argument that veterans are important	Show students the cover of the picture book *Veterans: Heroes in Our Neighborhood*. Tell them that this book is about veterans and that it will help them build knowledge about who is being honored in the photograph from the beginning of the unit. Use one or more of the four Ps of social studies prereading strategies (see chapter 4, page 81) before reading.

4	**Source:** Picture book—*Veterans: Heroes in Our Neighborhood* **Before-Reading Strategy:** Frayer Model **Purpose:** Build knowledge about the definition of *veteran*; provide evidence to support the argument that veterans are important	Build students' understanding of the vocabulary word *veteran* by completing a Frayer Model (see chapter 4, page 81) together as a class before reading.
5	**Source:** Picture book—*Veterans: Heroes in Our Neighborhood* **During-Reading Strategy:** Text structure graphic organizer—description **Purpose:** Build knowledge about the definition of *veteran*; provide evidence to support the argument that veterans are important	Use a description-text-structure graphic organizer (see chapter 4, page 81) during reading. Explain to students that authors of informational text organize it for readers so they can understand it easier. Tell them that this book is organized using a specific type of text structure called description. This means the author will provide a lot of facts and details about veterans. Show students a description graphic organizer and tell them that their job is to listen for descriptions about veterans while you are reading. Stop throughout the book and add details to the graphic organizer.
6	**Source:** Picture book—*Veterans: Heroes in Our Neighborhood* **After-Reading Strategy:** Five words **Purpose:** Build knowledge about the definition of *veteran*; provide evidence to support the argument that veterans are important	Return to the Frayer Model created in step 4 and revise if needed based on what students learned from the book after reading. Have students use the five words after-reading strategy (see chapter 4, page 81) to summarize the book while focusing on the importance of veterans.

continued ▶

Figure 5.2: Sample Veterans Day daily plans for grade 2.

	Day 2	
7	Show students the cover of the picture book *The Wall*. Tell them that this book is going to help them build more knowledge about where the event in the photograph from the beginning of the unit takes place. Use one or more of the four Ps of social studies prereading strategies (see chapter 4, page 81) before reading.	**Source:** Picture book—*The Wall* (Bunting, 2001) **Before-Reading Strategy:** Four Ps of social studies prereading **Purpose:** Build knowledge about the definition of *monument*; provide evidence to support the argument that monuments honor veterans' sacrifices
8	Assess students' prior knowledge before reading and prime their brains for learning about the Vietnam Veterans Memorial wall by using an anticipation guide (see chapter 4, page 81). Students complete the before-reading column before reading the text.	**Source:** Picture book—*The Wall* **Before-Reading Strategy:** Anticipation guide **Purpose:** Build knowledge about the definition of *monument*; provide evidence to support the argument that monuments honor veterans' sacrifices
9	Read small chunks of the text (see chapter 4, page 81) followed by a whole-group discussion that focuses on the main ideas from the anticipation guide. Have students return to the anticipation guide and complete the after-reading column.	**Source:** Picture Book—*The Wall* **During-Reading Strategy:** Chunking the text **Purpose:** Build knowledge about the definition of *monument*; provide evidence to support the argument that monuments honor veterans' sacrifices
10	Use the hot seat strategy (see chapter 4, page 81) after reading to help students begin to understand the sacrifices veterans make and how those sacrifices affect their families and friends.	**Source:** Picture book—*The Wall* **After-Reading Strategy:** Hot seat **Purpose:** Build knowledge about the definition of *monument*; provide evidence to support the argument that monuments honor veterans' sacrifices
11	Return to the photograph from step 1. Using information from the texts, have students explain where they think this photograph was taken and what is happening in the photograph. After the discussion, read the photograph title and caption to students. Use the historical thinking skills sourcing, contextualizing, and corroborating.	**Task:** Revisit the photograph from step 1

	Day 3
12	**Source:** Photographs—Soldiers Carry a Wounded Comrade Through a Swamp and American Reinforcements Arriving on the French Coast **Strategy:** Visual thinking **Purpose:** Build knowledge about what a soldier does; provide evidence to support the argument that soldiers are heroic	Give each student a copy of the photographs Soldiers Carry a Wounded Comrade Through a Swamp and American Reinforcements Arriving on the French Coast or project the photographs so everyone can see them. Don't tell the students the title of the photographs or provide any background information at this point in the lesson. Analyze the photographs using the visual thinking primary source analysis strategy (see chapter 3, page 47) with the focus of building students' understanding of the sacrifices that veterans make.
13	**Source:** Picture book—*Proud as a Peacock, Brave as a Lion* (Barclay, 2009) **Before-Reading Strategy:** Four Ps of social studies prereading **Purpose:** Provide evidence to support the argument that veterans are heroic, and we honor them with monuments	Show students the cover of the picture book *Proud as a Peacock, Brave as a Lion*. Explain that this book tells the story of a boy who is visiting a monument with his grandfather that honors veterans. Before they go to the monument, the little boy learns what his grandfather did as a soldier. Use one or more of the four Ps of social studies prereading strategies (see chapter 4, page 81) before reading.
14	**Source:** Picture book—*Proud as a Peacock, Brave as a Lion* **Before-Reading Strategy:** Frayer Model **Purpose:** Provide evidence to support the argument that veterans are heroic, and we honor them with monuments	Build students' understanding of the vocabulary word *monument* by completing a Frayer Model (see chapter 4, page 81) together as a class before reading.
15	**Source:** Picture book—*Proud as a Peacock, Brave as a Lion* **During-Reading Strategy:** Chunking the text **Purpose:** Provide evidence to support the argument that veterans are heroic, and we honor them with monuments	Build students' understanding of what a soldier does and why the monument at the end of the book is important by using the chunking the text strategy (see chapter 4, page 81).

continued ▲

16	**Source:** Picture book—*Proud as a Peacock, Brave as a Lion* **After-Reading Strategy:** Hot seat **Purpose:** Provide evidence to support the argument that veterans are heroic, and we honor them with monuments	After reading, use the hot seat strategy (see chapter 4, page 81) to help students continue building their understanding of the sacrifices veterans make, how it affects their families and friends, and the importance of honoring veterans through monuments.
17	**Task:** Revisit photographs from step 12	Return to the photographs from step 12. Make connections to the character in the book and how these actions might be considered heroic. Use the historical thinking skills of sourcing, contextualizing, and corroborating.
Day 4		
18	**Task:** Assessment	**Classroom-based assessment:** A whole-class discussion leads to drawing a claim to answer the compelling question, What is a hero? (see chapter 2, page 29) **Anticipated answer:** Students might draw a picture of a soldier and label it with the term *hero*.
Day 5		
19	**Task:** Doing social studies	**Doing social studies by taking informed action:** Students will write thank-you letters to soldiers through the organization Operation Gratitude.

Source	Purpose	Sequence
Photograph: Visitors Search for Names on the Vietnam Veterans Memorial (www.docsteach.org/documents/document/search-names-vietnam-memorial)	• Spark curiosity • Build knowledge about the memorial	1
Interview: Maya Lin, "Vietnam Veterans Memorial, 1982" (www.mayalinstudio.com/memory-works/vietnam-veterans-memorial)	• Provide evidence to support an argument about how people's perspectives influence their decisions	4
Letter: "Condolence Letter From President Kennedy to the McAndrews" (www.docsteach.org/documents/document/kennedy-condolence-mcandrew)	• Provide evidence to support an argument about how people's perspectives influence their decisions	6
Picture Book: Maya Lin: Artist-Architect of Light and Lines by Jeanne Walker Harvey (2017)	• Build knowledge about why the Vietnam Veterans Memorial wall was created • Provide evidence to support an argument about how people's perspectives influence their decisions	3
Informational Article: "Vietnam War" (History.com, 2024)	• Build knowledge about the Vietnam War	2
Picture Book: The Wall by Eve Bunting (2001)	• Build knowledge about the Vietnam Veterans Memorial wall • Provide evidence to support an argument about how people's perspectives influence their decisions	5

Figure 5.3: Sequencing sources in a Veterans Day unit for grade 5.

Step Number	Include the task, primary or secondary source and analysis strategy (from the 3–5 planning template example shown in figure 4.10, page 106), and purpose (from the planned sequencing for 3–5 example shown in figure 5.3, page 117)	Plan
		Day 1
1	**Source:** Photograph—Visitors Search for Names on the Vietnam Veterans Memorial **Strategy:** Jumping in **Purpose:** Spark curiosity; build knowledge about the memorial	Give each student a copy of the photograph Visitors Search for Names on the Vietnam Veterans Memorial or project the photograph so everyone can see it. Don't tell the students the title of the photograph or provide any background information at this point in the lesson. Analyze the photograph using the jumping in primary source analysis strategy (see chapter 3, page 47) to get students thinking about what they might see, hear, smell, or touch if they were present at this event. Ask students what they think is going on based on their observations after using the analysis strategy.
2	**Task:** Introduce the compelling question, How do people's perspectives influence their decisions?	Introduce the compelling question for your unit. Explain to students that the people in the photograph are visiting a monument that honors veterans. Tell them that they are going to look at some historical sources to learn more about this monument and why it was built.
3	**Source:** Informational article—"Vietnam War" (History.com, 2024) **Before-Reading Strategy:** Anticipation guide **Purpose:** Build knowledge about the Vietnam War	Build students' background knowledge using this source since most fifth graders have not studied the Vietnam War. Assess students' prior knowledge before reading and prime their brains for learning about the Vietnam War by using an anticipation guide (see chapter 4, page 81) and completing the before-reading column.

4	**Source:** Informational article—"Vietnam War" **During-Reading Strategy:** Text structure graphic organizer—description **Purpose:** Build knowledge about the Vietnam War	Use a description text structure graphic organizer (see chapter 4, page 81) while reading. Explain to students that authors of informational text organize it for readers so that they can understand it easier. Tell them that this article is organized using a specific type of text structure called description. This means the author will provide a lot of facts and details about the Vietnam War. Show students a description graphic organizer and tell them their job is to listen for facts and details about the war while you are reading. Explain that you will add characteristics to your graphic organizer as you are reading. Stop throughout the book and add details to the graphic organizer.
5	**Source:** Informational article—"Vietnam War" **After-Reading Strategy:** Five words **Purpose:** Build knowledge about the Vietnam War	Have students return to the anticipation guide from step 3 and complete the after-reading column. Then have students use the five words after-reading strategy (see chapter 4, page 81) to summarize the article while also focusing on the important details of the Vietnam War.
6	**Task:** Revisit the photograph from step 1	Revisit the photograph from step 1. Tell students that the people in the photograph are visiting the Vietnam Veterans Memorial wall. Discuss the question, How does knowing details about the war help you understand the reactions of the people visiting the wall? Use the historical thinking skills sourcing, contextualizing, and corroborating.

Figure 5.4: Sample Veterans Day daily plans for grade 5.

continued ▶

		Day 2
7	**Source:** Picture book—*Maya Lin: Artist-Architect of Light and Lines* (Harvey, 2017) **Before-Reading Strategy:** Four Ps of social studies prereading **Purpose:** Build knowledge about why the wall was created; provide evidence to support an argument about how people's perspectives influence their decisions	Show students the cover of the picture book *Maya Lin: Artist-Architect of Light and Lines*. Tell students that this book tells the story of the young woman who designed the Vietnam Veterans Memorial wall. Use one or more of the four Ps of social studies prereading strategies before reading.
8	**Source:** Picture book—*Maya Lin: Artist-Architect of Light and Lines* **Before-Reading Strategy:** Frayer Model **Purpose:** Build knowledge about why the wall was created; provide evidence to support an argument about how people's perspectives influence their decisions	Build students' understanding of the vocabulary word *memorial* by completing a Frayer Model (see chapter 4, page 81) together as a class before reading.
9	**Source:** Picture book—*Maya Lin: Artist-Architect of Light and Lines* **During-Reading Strategy:** Chunking the text **Purpose:** Build knowledge about why the wall was created; provide evidence to support an argument about how people's perspectives influence their decisions	Read small chunks of the text (see chapter 4, page 81) followed by a whole-group discussion that focuses on Maya Lin's perspectives and how those perspectives guided her decisions about the wall's design.
10	**Source:** Picture book—*Maya Lin: Artist-Architect of Light and Lines* **After-Reading Strategy:** Hot seat **Purpose:** Build knowledge about why the wall was created; provide evidence to support an argument about how people's perspectives influence their decisions	Use the hot seat strategy (see chapter 4, page 81) after reading to help students continue to build their understanding of Maya Lin's decisions regarding the wall's design.

Day 3

#	Source / Strategy / Purpose	Day 3
11	**Source:** Interview—Maya Lin, "Vietnam Veterans Memorial, 1982" **Strategy:** Ranking **Purpose:** Provide evidence to support an argument about how people's perspectives influence their decisions	Introduce the next primary source, which is an interview with Maya Lin. As students read the interview, they will underline important sentences regarding Maya Lin's decisions regarding the design of the wall. After reading the interview, they will use the primary source analysis strategy ranking (see chapter 3, page 47). Follow this up with a discussion about what information from the interview matched that in the picture book about Maya Lin and what information from the interview extended their understanding about Maya Lin's story. Use the historical thinking skill corroborating.
12	**Source:** Picture book—*The Wall* (Bunting, 2001) **Before-Reading Strategy:** Four Ps of social studies prereading **Purpose:** Build knowledge about the Vietnam Veterans Memorial wall; provide evidence to support an argument about how people's perspectives influence their decisions	Remind students that from the last two sources (the picture book and interview) they have learned that Maya Lin wanted the Vietnam Veterans Memorial wall to be focused on names so that people who visited the wall could remember, and she wanted the wall to be a place of honor for all veterans. Show students the cover of the picture book *The Wall*. As always, before reading, use one or more of the four Ps of social studies prereading strategies (see chapter 4, page 81). Tell students that the purpose for reading is to listen to determine whether the people who visit the wall in this book experience what Maya Lin hoped they would: remembrance and honor.
13	**Source:** Picture book—*The Wall* **During-Reading Strategy:** Text structure graphic organizer—cause and effect **Purpose:** Build knowledge about the Vietnam Veterans Memorial wall; provide evidence to support an argument about how people's perspectives influence their decisions	Use a cause-and-effect text structure graphic organizer (see chapter 4, page 81) during reading. Explain to students that authors of informational text organize their texts for readers so that they can understand it easier. Tell them that this book is organized using a specific type of text structure called cause and effect. This means the characters will say or do something that affects them. Sometimes this effect is an emotion and sometimes it is an action. Explain that you will add these causes and effects to your graphic organizer as you are reading. Stop throughout the book and add details to the graphic organizer.

continued ▲

14	**Source:** Picture book—*The Wall* **After-Reading Strategy:** Hot seat **Purpose:** Build knowledge about the Vietnam Veterans Memorial wall; provide evidence to support an argument about how people's perspectives influence their decisions	Use the hot seat strategy (see chapter 4, page 81) after reading to help students continue to build their understanding of the wall, why Maya Lin designed it the way she did, and how visitors feel when they visit the wall.
Day 4		
15	**Source:** Letter—"Condolence Letter From President Kennedy to the McAndrews" **Strategy:** Word-phrase-sentence **Purpose:** Provide evidence to support an argument about how people's perspectives influence their decisions	Give each student a copy of the primary source "Condolence Letter From President Kennedy to the McAndrews." Use the word-phrase-sentence primary source analysis strategy (see chapter 3, page 47) to guide students' thinking regarding how the family must have felt when they received this letter and the emotions they would feel when visiting the wall and seeing their son's name there. Use the historical thinking skills sourcing, close reading, and contextualizing.
Day 5		
16	**Task:** Assessment	**Classroom-based assessment:** Students will answer the compelling question (How do people's perspectives influence their decisions?) using the claims-evidence-reasoning framework in a written paragraph (see chapter 2, page 29). **Anticipated answers:** People create monuments because they think soldiers need to be honored. In the interview, Maya Lin said that she wanted people to be able to visit the monument and remember the names of people who fought in the war. This shows that she wanted the soldiers to be honored by putting their names on the memorial. Sometimes we make decisions because we feel like people need to be remembered. In the letter from President Kennedy to the parents of a fallen soldier during the Vietnam War, he said that the country was grateful for their son's contribution to the safety of the country. This shows that he wrote the letter because he wanted the soldier's sacrifice to be remembered.
Day 6		
17	**Task:** Doing social studies by taking informed action	**Doing social studies by taking informed action:** Students will write thank-you letters to soldiers through the organization Operation Gratitude.

Implementation Question and Answer

Now that you've seen how to turn the unit planning template into daily lessons, you might still have some questions. The following are implementation questions and answers.

Question: *I love this process, but I'm feeling overwhelmed! Where do I start?*

Answer: The best way is to start small. Don't try to reframe every unit that you teach. Choose one that is coming up soon and use the four-step planning process to design a unit with your team. If you do this with even one unit each quarter, you will have four revised units by the end of the year. You can build on it each year.

Another suggestion is to revise just one lesson instead of beginning with an entire unit. Choose a lesson that you already use and try adding a primary source and analysis strategy into that lesson to introduce the historical thinking skills. Find another primary source to use with another lesson and give yourself and your students the opportunity to practice the same strategies and skills. This enables you and your students to slowly master primary and secondary source analysis strategies. As you get comfortable with using strategies in individual lessons, you can then use them in more units.

One final suggestion is to start with a lesson that includes a picture book and one primary source that connects to that book—practice one day of a unit using this method. Over time, you can add additional lessons about that topic until you've created a unit. Before long, you'll become comfortable with historical thinking skills, primary sources, and analysis strategies, and it will become natural to embed these practices throughout your entire day.

Question: *I am required to use a district-adopted resource or textbook with a scripted scope and sequence. How can I use this planning process with resources I already have?*

Answer: You can still use the planning process and use the textbook or texts that come from the resource as secondary sources during step 4 of the planning process. Another suggestion is to find primary sources that are already in your resource or find primary sources from the list in chapter 3 (page 47) to use in tandem. By using the historical thinking skills and primary sources with analysis strategies, you are still teaching your students the skills and processes of social studies.

Question: *I don't have time to teach social studies as a separate subject during the day. Can I use this process during my ELA block?*

Answer: Yes! I suggest using this process to plan for social studies first and then adding extra steps to your daily lesson plans that focus on your ELA standards. For example, use the primary and secondary sources with the strategies outlined in this book, but return to those texts on separate days to focus on ELA standards. This way students are being given the opportunity to practice the skills and processes of both ELA and social studies.

Question: *I'm not confident in my own understanding of social studies concepts and events. How can I build my own content knowledge?*

Answer: In her book, *The Reading Comprehension Blueprint: Helping Students Make Meaning From Text*, literacy consultant Nancy L. Hennessy (2021) writes, "What educators know matters! Effective instruction depends on experience and explicit knowledge" (p. 8). This can be a scary thought for elementary teachers as many of us do not have majors or minors in history! A quick way that I have found to build my historical and social studies background knowledge is by looking at the background information provided in lesson plans geared for secondary students. These texts would be too difficult for elementary students but are a quick way for the teacher to learn more. Lessons found at https://teachinghistory.org, https://C3teachers.org, and https://inquirygroup.org often provide background-information paragraphs. Additional ideas for building content knowledge include listening to social studies–related podcasts, reading books about historical events, and participating in free webinars from places like the Library of Congress and the National Archives.

Summary

You have learned how to create social studies units for your elementary classroom using a four-step planning process throughout this book. The four steps are (1) Making Meaning of Social Studies Standards, (2) Creating Assessments, (3) Choosing and Analyzing Primary Sources, and (4) Choosing and Analyzing Secondary Sources. In this final chapter, you learned how to take your unit plan and turn it into daily lesson plans using the sequencing sources chart you created (see chapter 4, page 81) and your completed four-step unit planning template. We also looked at common implementation questions and answers that might come up as you begin to rethink social studies instruction in your elementary classroom.

Epilogue

I want to take you back to a cold December day in 1942. A young man, only twenty-one years old, has just enlisted in the United States Marine Corps. He will spend the next two and a half years in the South Pacific campaign of World War II. He will be part of the battles on the Marshall and Mariana Islands, including Saipan and Tinian. On one of these islands, he will suffer wounds that give him his first Purple Heart. Eventually, he will arrive on Iwo Jima, Japan, on February 19, 1945, where he will continue to fight until suffering more serious injuries on March 6, 1945. He will be sent home to recover, and the war will end before he is able to rejoin his division. He will be awarded a second Purple Heart for the injuries sustained on Iwo Jima.

This young man, my grandfather, was involved in three of the largest battles of the South Pacific, yet he never spoke much about his time during the war. Although he was proud to be a Marine, I don't think he ever considered himself a hero. But to me, and most Americans, he is—and will always be—a hero. A member of the Greatest Generation, a name given in "tribute to the resilience and patriotic spirit of those who lived through the Great Depression and then fought in World War II," he and many others deserve to be remembered (Kagan, 2024).

The lessons highlighted throughout this book have been on the topic of Veterans Day and honoring those who have served their country. These lessons are a tribute to my grandfather and a reminder of the importance of not just knowing history but thinking like historians. Consider this quote from Stanford University (n.d.):

> For a great many people, history is a set of facts, a collection of events, a series of things that happened, one after another, in the past. In fact, history is far more than these things—it is a way of thinking about and seeing the world.

The events of the past will always influence the events of the present.

We live in a time where conversations about history, social studies, and civics can become very contentious. That is why it is so important to teach our students how to study primary sources and find the historical details written by those who were there—not change it to match the social and political agendas of today. Our goal should not be to change history, but to learn from it.

The sacrifices made by my grandfather, and many, many others before and after him, cannot be forgotten. We must work to preserve and protect the democratic values the United States was founded on and remember those, like my grandfather, who have sacrificed so much for it. My hope is that with this easy, four-step process, you will be equipped to teach social studies every day, even to our youngest elementary learners. Let these words of Abraham Lincoln, spoken on August 22, 1864, inspire your journey: "It is not merely for to-day, but for all time to come that we should perpetuate for our children's children this great and free government, which we have enjoyed all our lives" (AbrahamLincoln.org, n.d.).

Appendix A

Appendix A includes blank planning templates to use as you create your own social studies units, including "The Four-Step Planning Process Template".

The Four-Step Planning Process Template

Topic or Unit:	

Step 1: Making Meaning of Standards

Standard:

Enduring Understanding:

Compelling Question:

Step 2: Creating Assessments

Classroom-Based Assessment:

Doing Social Studies:

Step 3: Choosing and Analyzing Primary Sources

Step 4: Choosing and Analyzing Secondary Sources

The Frayer Model Template

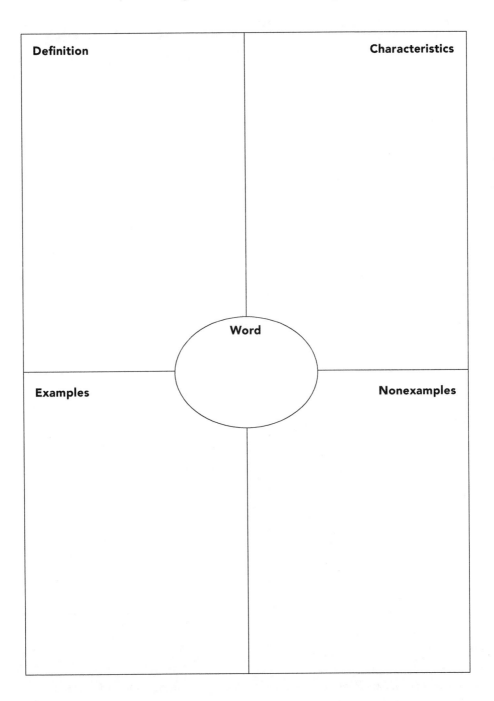

Definition

Characteristics

Word

Examples

Nonexamples

Vocabulary Knowledge Rating Scale

Word	I Know It Well 1	I Have Seen or Heard It 2	I Have No Clue 3

Source: Adapted from Reading Rockets. (n.d.). Classroom strategies: Inferencing. *Accessed at https://readingrockets.org/classroom/classroom-strategies/inferencing on October 31, 2023.*

Sequencing Sources Chart

Source	Purpose	Sequence

Appendix B

Completed Planning Templates

Appendix B contains four completed unit templates: two for grades K–2 and two for grades 3–5. Each template begins with an overview of the unit, which includes explanations of the following: the unit topic, the discipline-specific content that will be covered, the primary and secondary sources that will be used, the enduring understanding, the compelling question and class-room-based assessment idea to assess the compelling question, and an idea for doing social studies. After the overview, there is a completed unit planning template that also includes the standard and the specific analysis strategies you can use with the primary and secondary sources. Please note that these unit plans are built around standards from the C3 Framework. For this reason, you may choose to use the unit plan as is, you might use bits and pieces that work for you and your students, you may need to revise these plans to match your standards, or you may need to simply replace the C3 Framework standard with a comparable one from your district's standards document.

Sample Grades K–2
Completed Planning Template: Rules

This unit for K–2 focuses on the civics topic of *rules*. At the end of the unit, students will have the enduring understanding that good citizens follow the rules. The historical sources include photographs, informational articles, and a picture book that focus on students as citizens of their classroom, and, therefore, they must follow the rules in their classroom. They will analyze a photograph of students playing on a playground, a photograph of students sitting quietly in a classroom, and a photograph of students working together to study a map to provide evidence that following rules keeps students safe and enables them to learn. They will also read or listen to informational articles about the importance of rules at school and a picture book about a young boy who learns the importance of following rules because there are consequences when he doesn't. Students will demonstrate their understanding by using drawings to answer the compelling question, Why should we follow rules? Students will draw two pictures: the first one of themselves following a rule at home or school and the second one of themselves *not* following a rule at home or school. Students will practice doing social studies by working with the teacher to create a set of classroom rules.

Topic or Unit:	Rules

Step 1: Making Meaning of Standards

Standard: D2.Civ.3.K-2. Explain the need for and purposes of rules in various settings inside and outside of school.

Enduring Understanding: Good citizens follow the rules.

Compelling Question: Why should we follow rules?

Step 2: Creating Assessments

Classroom-Based Assessment: Students will draw two pictures: the first one of themselves following a rule at home or school and the second one of themselves not following a rule at home or school.

Doing Social Studies: Work together to create the rules for your classroom.

Step 3: Choosing and Analyzing Primary Sources

Primary Source and Close Reading Strategy:

- Photograph: Open Air School, Providence
  (www.loc.gov/item/2014680223)
  - Close Reading Strategy: Hide-and-Seek
- Photograph: Nursery School Playground
  (www.loc.gov/item/2017775432)
  - Close Reading Strategy: Zoom In
- Photograph: Greenbelt School Children Studying Map
  (www.loc.gov/item/2017777354)
  - Close Reading Strategy: What Would You Ask?

Making Time for Social Studies © 2025 Solution Tree Press • SolutionTree.com
Visit **go.SolutionTree.com/instruction** to download this free reproducible.

Step 4: Choosing and Analyzing Secondary Sources

Secondary Source and Before-, During-, and After-Reading Strategies:

- Informational article: "Playing by the Rules" (Textproject.org, n.d.b)
  - Before: Frayer Model
  - During: Text structure graphic organizer—compare and contrast
  - After: Inside-outside circle
- Informational article: "Who Is a Good Citizen at School?" (ReadWorks, n.d.a)
  - Before: Frayer Model
  - During: Text structure graphic organizer—description
  - After: Five words
- Informational article: "Why Do We Need Rules?" (ReadWorks, n.d.b)
  - Before: Anticipation guide
  - During: Text structure graphic organizer—cause and effect
  - After: Five words
- Picture book: *David Goes to School* by David Shannon (1999)
  - Before: Vocabulary knowledge rating
  - During: Thinking job
  - After: Hot seat

Source for standard: National Council for the Social Studies. (2013). College, career, and civic life (C3) framework for social studies state standards: Guidance for enhancing the rigor of K–12 civics, economics, geography, and history. Silver Spring, MD: Author. Accessed at https://socialstudies.org/system/files/2022/c3-framework-for-social-studies-rev0617.2.pdf on March 13, 2023.

References

ReadWorks. (n.d.a). *Who is a good citizen at school?* Accessed at www.readworks.org /article/Community-Life/085bb0dc-6609-41e7-92e2-43a4c6185bf9#!articleTab:content /contentSection:d53a36e0-d740-4321-b6a8-1bb466e03b78 on August 13, 2024.

ReadWorks. (n.d.b). *Why do we need rules?* Accessed at www.readworks.org/article /Community-Life/085bb0dc-6609-41e7-92e2-43a4c6185bf9#!articleTab:content /contentSection:39180fc3-9d95-44e7-b220-9383a0634130 on August 13, 2024.

Shannon, D. (1999). *David goes to school.* New York: Blue Sky Press.

Textproject.org. (n.d.b). *Playing by the rules.* Accessed at https://textproject.org/wp-content /uploads/fyi4k/FYI-for-Kids-4-15-play-by-the-rules.pdf on August 13, 2024.

Sample Grades K–2
Completed Planning Template:
Then and Now

This unit for K–2 focuses on the history topic of *then and now*. The historical content of this unit focuses on two women, Mary Lemist Titcomb and Anne Carroll Moore, who were both instrumental in changing how young children were able to access books and libraries. Anne Carroll Moore advocated for children's spaces in public libraries at a time when children under the age of fourteen weren't even allowed in libraries. Students will analyze a photograph of her, read several newspaper articles about her, and read a picture book that tells her story. Mary Lemist Titcomb created the first bookmobile to provide people of all ages and backgrounds access to books. Students will analyze a photograph of her and several photographs of bookmobiles through the years, read several newspaper articles about her, and read an informational article about the history of bookmobiles.

Students will also read an informational article about a modern-day fifth grader who collects books and gives them away to children who don't have access. At the end of the unit, students will have the enduring understanding that children in the past lived differently than children today. Students will demonstrate their understanding using drawings and a claim statement to answer the compelling question, How does when you live impact how you live? For example, students might draw a picture of children checking out books from a bookmobile with the claim statement, *If you lived long ago, you might have gotten your books from a bookmobile instead of the library.* Students will practice doing social studies by organizing and building a Little Free Library (https://littlefreelibrary.org/about) in their community, or they can organize a donation drive for providing new books if their community already has a Little Free Library.

Topic or Unit:	Then and Now
Step 1: Making Meaning of Standards	
Standard: D2.His.2.K-2. Compare life in the past to life today.	
Enduring Understanding: Children in the past lived differently than children today.	
Compelling Question: How does when you live impact how you live?	
Step 2: Creating Assessments	
Classroom-Based Assessment: The teacher will guide a whole-class discussion that will lead to a claim. Students will draw a picture with details from the sources and write the claim underneath their picture.	
Doing Social Studies: Students can organize a Little Free Library (https://littlefreelibrary.org) in their community, or they can organize a donation drive for providing new books if their community already has a Little Free Library.	

Step 3: Choosing and Analyzing Primary Sources

Primary Source and Close Reading Strategy:

- Newspaper article about Mary Lemist Titcomb: "Horse and Buggy Days" (Hagerstown Globe, 1942)
    - Close Reading Strategy: Word-Phrase-Sentence
- Newspaper article about Mary Lemist Titcomb's Bookmobile: "An R. F. D. Library Service" (Bryan Daily Eagle and Pilot, 1915)
    - Close Reading Strategy: Annotation
- Newspaper article about Anne Carroll Moore: "Continuing a Tradition" (Daily Monitor, 1941)
    - Close Reading Strategy: Word-Phrase-Sentence
- Newspaper article about the importance of Anne Carroll Moore's work: "Books for Young America" (Fuller, 1932)
    - Close Reading Strategy: Annotation
- Photograph of Anne Carroll Moore: https://tinyurl.com/bdd8d5sn
    - Close Reading Strategy: Strike a Pose
- Photograph of Mary Lemist Titcomb: https://msa.maryland.gov/msa/educ /exhibits/womenshallfame/html/titcomb.html
    - Close Reading Strategy: What Would You Ask?
- Photograph collection of bookmobiles: https://archiveproject.com/history-bookmobile-library-old-photos
    - Close Reading Strategy: Caption Matching

Step 4: Choosing and Analyzing Secondary Sources

Secondary Source and Before-, During-, and After-Reading Strategies:

- Picture book: *Library on Wheels: Mary Lemist Titcomb and America's First Book Mobile* by Sharlee Glenn (2018)
    - Before: Linking language
    - During: Chunking the text
    - After: Writing questions
- Picture book: *Miss Moore Thought Otherwise: How Anne Carroll Moore Created Libraries for Children* by Jan Pinborough (2013)
    - Before: Vocabulary knowledge rating
    - During: Chunking the text
    - After: Hot seat
- Informational article: "A Hero Who Gives Things Away" (Textproject.org, n,d,c)
    - Before: Frayer Model
    - During: Thinking job
    - After: Five words
- Informational article: "A Brief History of Bookmobiles" (Chemung County Library District, 2020)
    - Before: Linking language
    - During: Text structure graphic organizer—description
    - After: Five words

Source for standard: National Council for the Social Studies. (2013). College, career, and civic life (C3) framework for social studies state standards: Guidance for enhancing the rigor of K–12 civics, economics, geography, and history. *Silver Spring, MD: Author. Accessed at https://socialstudies.org/system/files/2022/c3-framework-for-social-studies-rev0617.2.pdf on March 13, 2023.*

page 2 of 3

References

Bryan Daily Eagle and Pilot. (1915, December 16). *An R. F. D. library service.* Accessed at https://chroniclingamerica.loc.gov/lccn/sn86088651/1915-12-16/ed-1/seq-3 on August 13, 2024.

Chemung County Library District. (2020, October 5). *A brief history of bookmobiles.* Accessed at https://ccld.lib.ny.us/2020/10/05/a-brief-history-of-bookmobiles on August 13, 2024.

Daily Monitor. (1941, September 11). *Continuing a tradition.* Accessed at https://chroniclingamerica.loc.gov/lccn/sn96077287/1941-09-11/ed-1/seq-4/ on August 13, 2024.

Fuller, A. D. (1932, November 17). *Books for young America. Marion Progress.* Accessed at https://chroniclingamerica.loc.gov/lccn/sn91068695/1932-11-17/ed-1/seq-4/ on August 13, 2024.

Glenn, S. (2018). *Library on wheels: Mary Lemist Titcomb and America's first bookmobile.* New York: Abrams Books for Young Readers.

Hagerstown Globe. (1942, July 10). *Horse and buggy days.* Accessed at https://chroniclingamerica.loc.gov/lccn/sn89060186/1942-07-10/ed-1/seq-3/ on August 13, 2024.

Pinborough, J. (2013). *Miss Moore thought otherwise: How Anne Carroll Moore created libraries for children* (D. Atwell, Illus.). New York: Houghton Mifflin Harcourt.

Textproject.org. (n.d.c). *A hero who gives things away.* Accessed at https://textproject.org/wp-content/uploads/fyi4k/FYI-for-Kids-1-15-A-hero-who-gives-things-away.pdf on August 13, 2024.

Sample Grades 3–5
Completed Planning Template: Inventions

This unit for grades 3–5 focuses on the civics topic of *inventions*. At the end of the unit, students will have the enduring understanding that sometimes inventions occur accidentally while people are trying to solve problems. The historical sources include newspaper articles, photographs, informational articles, and picture books that focus on the history of three accidental inventions: (1) the Band-Aid®, (2) the chocolate chip cookie, and (3) bubble gum. Each of these historical sources guides students toward understanding why the inventions came about and how they changed society. Students will demonstrate their understanding by creating storyboards to answer the compelling question, How do inventions change a society? Students will choose one of the inventions and create a storyboard about it. In their storyboard, they will show how that invention affected the inventor's life and how it affected society at large. Students will explain their storyboards with their reasoning in an oral presentation. Students will practice doing social studies by creating an invention to solve a problem in their school or community. Students will then present their invention to a group of school or community members.

Topic or Unit:	Accidental Inventions

Step 1: Making Meaning of Standards

Standard: D2.Civ.14.3-5. Illustrate historical and contemporary means of changing society.

Enduring Understanding: Sometimes inventions occur because people are trying to solve a problem.

Compelling Question: How do inventions change a society?

Step 2: Creating Assessments

Classroom-Based Assessment: Students create a storyboard to represent their claim in pictures, labeling their claim and evidence with sources. During an oral discussion or presentation, students explain their storyboard, identify their evidence and sources within the storyboard, and explain how their evidence supports the claim (reasoning).

Doing Social Studies: Students will create an invention to solve a problem in their school or community. Students will then present their invention to a group of school or community members.

Making Time for Social Studies © 2025 Solution Tree Press • SolutionTree.com
Visit **go.SolutionTree.com/instruction** to download this free reproducible.

Step 3: Choosing and Analyzing Primary Sources

Primary Source and Close Reading Strategy:
- Newspaper ad for Band-Aids (Johnson & Johnson, 1931)
  - Close Reading Strategy: Matching Captions
- Newspaper ad for Band-Aids (Johnson & Johnson, 1932)
  - Close Reading Strategy: Matching Captions
- Newspaper ad for Band-Aids (Johnson & Johnson, 1940)
  - Close Reading Strategy: Matching Captions
- Photograph of Ruth Wakefield:
  www.digitalcommonwealth.org/search/commonwealth:5425kp84f
  - Close Reading Strategy: What Would You Ask?
- Trade card for the Toll House:
  www.historicnewengland.org/explore/collections-access/gusn/249044
  - Close Reading Strategy: Thirty-Second Look
- Newspaper ad for a cookbook:
  https://chroniclingamerica.loc.gov/lccn/sn83045462/1945-12-02/ed-1/
  seq-127
  - Close Reading Strategy: Student-Generated Questions

Step 4: Choosing and Analyzing Secondary Sources

Secondary Source and Before-, During-, and After-Reading Strategies:

- Picture book: *The Boo-Boos That Changed the World: A True Story About an Accidental Invention (Really!)* by Barry Wittenstein (2018)
  - Before: Linking language
  - During: Chunking the text
  - After: Writing questions
- Picture book: *How the Cookie Crumbled: The True (and Not-So-True) Stories of the Invention of the Chocolate Chip Cookie* by Gilbert Ford (2017)
  - Before: Vocabulary knowledge rating
  - During: Text structure graphic organizer—sequence
  - After: Hot seat
- Informational article: "Inventing Bubble Gum"
  www.commonlit.org/en/texts/inventing-bubble-gum
  - Before: Linking language
  - During: Text structure graphic organizer—cause and effect
  - After: Five words

Source for standard: National Council for the Social Studies. (2013). College, career, and civic life (C3) framework for social studies state standards: Guidance for enhancing the rigor of K–12 civics, economics, geography, and history. *Silver Spring, MD: Author. Accessed at https://socialstudies.org/system/files/2022/c3-framework-for-social-studies-rev0617.2.pdf on March 13, 2023.*

References

Ford, G. (2017). *How the cookie crumbled: The true (and not-so-true) stories of the invention of the chocolate chip cookie.* New York: Atheneum Books for Young Readers.

Johnson & Johnson. (1931, October 2). *Stock your cabinet with reliable Johnson and Johnson products.* Evening Star, C-7. Accessed at https://chroniclingamerica.loc.gov/lccn /sn83045462/1931-10-02/ed-1/seq-39 on August 13, 2024.

Johnson & Johnson. (1932, June 1). *Johnson & Johnson first aid supplies.* Evening Star, A-11. Accessed at https://chroniclingamerica.loc.gov/lccn/sn83045462/1932-06-01/ed-1 /seq-11 on August 13, 2024.

Johnson & Johnson. (1940, January 21). [Advertisement for Band-Aid adhesive bandages]. Evening Star, 8. Accessed at https://chroniclingamerica.loc.gov/lccn/sn83045462/1940 -01-21/ed-1/seq-100/ on August 13, 2024.

Wittenstein, B. (2018). *The boo-boos that changed the world: A true story about an accidental invention (really!)* (C. Hsu, Illus.). Watertown, MA: Charlesbridge.

Sample Grades 3–5
Completed Planning Template: Civic Duty

This unit for grades 3–5 focuses on the topic of *civic duty*. The historical content of this unit focuses on the story of a young girl named Ruby Bridges, a woman named Susanna Salter, and a group of college students who participated in the first successful lunch-counter sit-in. Students will read a picture book about and written by Ruby Bridges to build content knowledge about her experience as the first Black child to integrate in a school system in the South in 1960. Students will also analyze a photograph of her during this event. Students will also learn about Susanna Salter, who was the first woman mayor. They will read a newspaper article written sixty-nine years after her election in which she is interviewed. Students will also read a picture book about Susanna being elected mayor and analyze two photographs of her: one taken around the time she became mayor and one taken several decades later. Students will also learn about the first lunch-counter sit-in, which took place at Dockum Drug Store in Wichita, Kansas. Students will analyze photographs of the drugstore, the sit-in, and a banner commemorating the fiftieth anniversary of the event. Students will also read a picture book about the Dockum Drug Store sit-in.

Students will also read an informational article about the importance of one civic duty: voting. At the end of the unit, students will have the enduring understanding that citizens' active participation is important, no matter your age, as they will have seen people of varying ages making a difference in their communities. Students will demonstrate their understanding by using the news reports activity to answer the compelling question, How does a citizen effect change in their community? For example, students can work in groups to create a news show script and then act it out. Their claim might be, *Citizens effect change in their community when they work to change laws.* The news show might include interviews with historical figures from the unit as well as local community members. Their script must include evidence from the sources with reasoning that connects the evidence to the claim. Students will practice doing social studies by creating a public service announcement encouraging their community members to participate in their local governments (for example, school board meetings and local elections) that can be posted on their school's social media accounts.

Topic or Unit:	Civic Duty

Step 1: Making Meaning of Standards

Standard: D2.Civ.2.3-5. Explain how a democracy relies on people's responsible participation and draw implications for how individuals should participate.

Enduring Understanding: The active participation of each citizen is important no matter their age.

Compelling Question: How does a citizen effect change in their community?

Step 2: Creating Assessments

Classroom-Based Assessment: Students will work in small groups to create a news show that answers their compelling question.

Doing Social Studies: Students will create a public service announcement encouraging their community members to participate in their local government that can be posted on their school's social media accounts.

Step 3: Choosing and Analyzing Primary Sources

Primary Source and Close Reading Strategy:

- Picture book (autobiography): *I Am Ruby Bridges* by Ruby Bridges (2022)
  - Close Reading Strategy: Ranking
- Photograph of Ruby Bridges:
  www.amightygirl.com/blog?p=26000
  - Close Reading Strategy: Strike a Pose
- Photograph in front of Dockum Drug Store:
  www.kshs.org/kansapedia/dockum-drug-store-sit-in/17048
  - Close Reading Strategy: Thinking Routine
- Photograph of the Dockum Sit-In:
  www.visitwichita.com/blog/post/
  dockum-drugstore-sit-in-why-it-matters-to-wichitas-rich-cultural-history
  - Close Reading Strategy: Thinking Routine
- Photograph of Dockum Sit-In banner:
  www.kshs.org/kansapedia/civil-rights-banner/15637
  - Close Reading Strategy: Thinking Routine
- Photograph of empty Dockum Drug Store:
  www.today.com/news/trailblazers-historic-1958-kansas-sit-share-their-stories-sheinelle-jones-t207474
  - Close Reading Strategy: Thinking Routine
- Newspaper article about Susanna Salter: "Town Recalls Election of First Woman Mayor" (Evening Star, 1956)
  - Close Reading Strategy: Word-Phrase-Sentence
- Photographs of Susanna Salter (younger and older):
  https://tinyurl.com/s8mj33vu
  - Close Reading Strategy: Strike a Pose with What Would You Ask?

Step 4: Choosing and Analyzing Secondary Sources

Secondary Source and Before-, During-, and After-Reading Strategies:

- Picture book: *A Vote for Susanna: The First Woman Mayor* by Karen M. Greenwald (2021)
    - Before: Linking language
    - During: Chunking the text
    - After: Hot seat
- Picture book: *People, Pride, and Promise: The Story of the Dockum Sit-In* by Prisca Barnes (2020)
    - Before: Vocabulary knowledge rating
    - During: Chunking the text
    - After: Hot seat
- Informational article: "Voting Makes a Difference" (Textproject.org, n.d.d)
    - Before: Anticipation guide
    - During: Thinking job
    - After: Five words

Source for standard: National Council for the Social Studies. (2013). College, career, and civic life (C3) framework for social studies state standards: Guidance for enhancing the rigor of K–12 civics, economics, geography, and history. *Silver Spring, MD: Author. Accessed at https://socialstudies.org/system/files/2022/c3-framework-for-social-studies-rev0617.2.pdf on March 13, 2023.*

References

Barnes, P. (2020). *People, pride, and promise: The story of the Dockum sit-in.* Wichita, KS: Storytime Village.

Bridges, R. (2022). *I am Ruby Bridges.* New York: Orchard Books.

Evening Star. (1956, April 4). *Town recalls election of first woman mayor.* Accessed at https://chroniclingamerica.loc.gov/lccn/sn83045462/1956-04-04/ed-1/seq-16 on August 13, 2024.

Greenwald, K. M. (2021). *A vote for Susanna: The first woman mayor* (S. James, Illus.). Chicago: Whitman.

Textproject.org. (n.d.d) *Voting makes a difference.* Accessed at https://textproject.org/wp-content/uploads/fyi4k/FYI-for-Kids-1-10-Voting-makes-a-difference.pdf on August 13, 2024.

References and Resources

AbrahamLincoln.org. (n.d.). *Abraham Lincoln quotes.* Accessed at https://abrahamlincoln.org /features/speeches-writings/abraham-lincoln-quotes on January 16, 2024.

AdLit. (n.d.). *Reading and writing strategies.* Accessed at www.adlit.org/in-the-classroom /strategies on November 20, 2023.

Ainsworth, L. (2015a, February 24). *Priority standards: The power of focus.* Accessed at https://edweek.org/teaching-learning/opinion-priority-standards-the-power-of-focus /2015/02 on September 16, 2023.

Ainsworth, L. (2015b, March 25). *Unwrapping the standards: A simple way to deconstruct learning outcomes.* Accessed at https://edweek.org/education/opinion-unwrapping-the -standards-a-simple-way-to-deconstruct-learning-outcomes/2015/03 on September 16, 2023.

Ainsworth, L., & Donovan, K. (2019). *Rigorous curriculum design: How to create curricular units of study that align standards, instruction, and assessment* (2nd ed.). Rexford, NY: International Center for Leadership in Education.

Altieri, J. L. (2016). *Reading science: Practical strategies for integrating instruction.* Portsmouth, NH: Heinemann.

Annenberg Classroom. (n.d.). *Civic education.* Accessed at www.annenbergclassroom.org /glossary_term/civic-education on May 8, 2024.

Argentar, D. M., Gillies, K. A. N., Rubenstein, M. M., & Wise, B. R. (2020). In M. Onuscheck & J. Spiller (Eds.), *Reading and writing strategies for the secondary science classroom in a PLC at Work.* Bloomington, IN: Solution Tree Press.

Argentar, D. M., Gillies, K. A. N., Rubenstein, M. M., & Wise, B. R. (2021). In M. Onuscheck & J. Spiller (Eds.), *Reading and writing strategies for the secondary social studies classroom in a PLC at Work.* Bloomington, IN: Solution Tree Press.

Arkansas Department of Education. (2022). *Grades K–4 social studies academic standards & disciplinary concepts* (Rev.). Accessed at https://dese.ade.arkansas.gov/Files/AR_Grades _K-4_Social_Studies_Standards_2022_LS.pdf on April 23, 2023.

Bailey, K., & Jakicic, C. (2023). *Common formative assessment: A toolkit for Professional Learning Communities at Work* (2nd ed.). Bloomington, IN: Solution Tree Press.

Barclay, J. (2009). *Proud as a peacock, brave as a lion*. Toronto, Ontario, Canada: Tundra Books.

Barnes, P. (2020). *People, pride, and promise: The story of the Dockum sit-in*. Wichita, KS: Storytime Village.

Bell, D. (2016, March 16). *Reading portraits: Analyzing art as a primary source* [Blog post]. Accessed at https://blogs.loc.gov/teachers/2016/03/reading-portraits-analyzing-art-as-a-primary-source on March 25, 2023.

Bloom, B. S. (Ed.). (1956). *Taxonomy of educational objectives: The classification of educational goals; Handbook I: Cognitive domain*. New York: McKay.

Bober, T. (2019). *Elementary educator's guide to primary sources: Strategies for teaching*. Santa Barbara, CA: ABC-CLIO.

Bridges, R. (2022). *I am Ruby Bridges*. New York: Orchard Books.

Brunsell, E. (2012, September 25). *Designing science inquiry: Claim + evidence + reasoning = explanation* [Blog post]. Accessed at https://edutopia.org/blog/science-inquiry-claim-evidence-reasoning-eric-brunsell on October 15, 2023.

Bryan Daily Eagle and Pilot. (1915, December 16). *An R. F. D. library service*. Accessed at https://chroniclingamerica.loc.gov/lccn/sn86088651/1915-12-16/ed-1/seq-3 on August 13, 2024.

Bunting, E. (2001). *The wall*. New York: Clarion Books.

Carrillo, S. (2023, May 3). *History and civics scores drop for U.S. eighth-graders on national test* [Radio broadcast]. Accessed at https://npr.org/2023/05/03/1173432887/history-and-civics-scores-drop-for-u-s-eighth-graders-on-national-test on August 27, 2023.

Catts, H. W. (2021–2022, Winter). *Rethinking how to promote reading comprehension*. Accessed at https://aft.org/ae/winter2021-2022/catts on April 23, 2023.

Cervetti, G. N., Wright, T. S., & Hwang, H. (2016). Conceptual coherence, comprehension, and vocabulary acquisition: A knowledge effect? *Reading and Writing: An Interdisciplinary Journal, 29*(4), 761–779.

Chemung County Library District. (2020, October 5). *A brief history of bookmobiles*. Accessed at https://ccld.lib.ny.us/2020/10/05/a-brief-history-of-bookmobiles on August 13, 2024.

Clowes, G. (2011). *The essential 5: A starting point for Kagan Cooperative Learning*. San Clemente, CA: Kagan Publishing. Accessed at https://kaganonline.com/free_articles/research_and_rationale/330/The-Essential-5-A-Starting-Point-for-Kagan-Cooperative-Learning on April 23, 2023.

Colorado Department of Education. (2020, August 27). *Developing disciplinary literacy in social studies*. Accessed at https://cde.state.co.us/cosocialstudies/ssliteracy on January 16, 2024.

Council of Chief State School Officers. (2018). *The marginalization of social studies.* Washington, DC: Author. Accessed at https://ccsso.org/sites/default/files/2018-11 /Elementary%20SS%20Brief%2045%20Minute%20Version_0.pdf on March 12, 2024.

Daily Monitor. (1941, September 11). *Continuing a tradition.* Accessed at https://chroniclingamerica.loc.gov/lccn/sn96077287/1941-09-11/ed-1/seq-4/ on August 13, 2024.

Diesen, D. (2020). *Equality's call: The story of voting rights in America* (M. Mora, Illus.). New York: Beach Lane Books.

Digital Inquiry Group. (n.d.). *Reading like a historian.* Accessed at https://inquirygroup.org /history-lessons on March 12, 2024.

Diliberti, M. K., Woo, A., & Kaufman, J. H. (2023, March 7). *The missing infrastructure for elementary (K–5) social studies instruction* [Research report RR-A134-17]. Accessed at https://rand.org/pubs/research_reports/RRA134-17.html on March 13, 2023.

Docsteach.org. (n.d.). *Letter from Kelli Middlestead about the Exxon Valdez oil spill.* Accessed at https://docsteach.org/documents/document/letter-from-kelli-middlestead on August 2, 2024.

Dotson, J. M. (2001). *Cooperative learning structures can increase student achievement.* Accessed at https://kaganonline.com/free_articles/research_and_rationale/increase _achievement.php on April 16, 2023.

Dougherty Stahl, K. A., & Bravo, M. A. (2010, April). Contemporary classroom vocabulary assessment for content areas. *The Reading Teacher, 63*(7), 566–578.

Driscoll, T., & McCusker, S. W. (2022). *Becoming active citizens: Practices to engage students in civic education across the curriculum.* Bloomington, IN: Solution Tree Press.

Easton, L. B. (2015). The art of dialogue. *Educational Leadership, 72*(7).

Edutopia. (2018, November 16). *Encouraging academic conversations with talk moves* [Video file]. Accessed at https://edutopia.org/video/encouraging-academic-conversations-talk -moves on June 21, 2023.

Evening Star. (1956, April 4). *Town recalls election of first woman mayor.* Accessed at https://chroniclingamerica.loc.gov/lccn/sn83045462/1956-04-04/ed-1/seq-16 on August 13, 2024.

Fisher, D., & Frey, N. (2014). *Checking for understanding: Formative assessment techniques for your classroom* (2nd ed.). Arlington, VA: ASCD.

Flygare, J., Hoegh, J. K., & Heflebower, T. (2022). *Planning and teaching in the standards-based classroom.* Bloomington, IN: Marzano Resources.

Fogarty, R. J., Kerns, G. M., & Pete, B. M. (2021). *Literacy reframed: How a focus on decoding, vocabulary, and background knowledge improves reading comprehension.* Bloomington, IN: Solution Tree Press.

Ford, G. (2017). *How the cookie crumbled: The true (and not-so-true) stories of the invention of the chocolate chip cookie.* New York: Atheneum Books for Young Readers.

Fuller, A. D. (1932, November 17). Books for young America. *Marion Progress*. Accessed at https://chroniclingamerica.loc.gov/lccn/sn91068695/1932-11-17/ed-1/seq-4 on August 13, 2024.

Garrison, S. (2016, September 23). *What are "text sets," and why use them in the classroom?* Accessed at https://fordhaminstitute.org/national/commentary/what-are-text-sets-and -why-use-them-classroom on May 7, 2023.

Glenn, S. (2018). *Library on wheels: Mary Lemist Titcomb and America's first bookmobile*. New York: Abrams Books for Young Readers.

Grant, S. G. (2013). *What are compelling questions?* Accessed at https://c3teachers.org/what -are-compelling-questions on April 18, 2023.

Greenwald, K. M. (2021). *A vote for Susanna: The first woman mayor* (S. James, Illus.). Chicago: Whitman.

Guilfoile, L., & Delander, B. (2014, January). *Guidebook: Six proven practices for effective civic learning*. Accessed at www.ecs.org/clearinghouse/01/10/48/11048.pdf on October 7, 2023.

Haass, R. (2023). *Why we need civics: We're failing to teach what it means to be American*. Accessed at https://theatlantic.com/ideas/archive/2023/01/american-identity-democracy -civics-education-requirement/672789 on May 14, 2023.

Hagerstown Globe. (1942, July 10). *Horse and buggy days*. Accessed at https://chronicling america.loc.gov/lccn/sn89060186/1942-07-10/ed-1/seq-3 on August 13, 2024.

Harvey, J. W. (2017). *Maya Lin: Artist-architect of light and lines*. New York: Holt.

Hennessy, N. L. (2021). *The reading comprehension blueprint: Helping students make meaning from text*. Baltimore: Brookes.

Hirsch, R. E. (2018). *The monarchs are missing: A butterfly mystery*. Minneapolis, MN: Millbrook Press.

History.com. (2024, May 16). *Vietnam War*. Accessed at www.history.com/topics /vietnam-war/vietnam-war-history on August 16, 2024.

Hochman, J. C., & Wexler, N. (2017). *The writing revolution: A guide to advancing thinking through writing in all subjects and grades*. San Francisco: Jossey-Bass.

Honore, S. A. (2022, April 15). *Picture books to expand thinking in the social studies classroom* [Blog post]. Accessed at https://socialstudies.com/blog/picture-books-to-use-in-the-social -studies-classroom on November 18, 2023.

iCivics. (n.d.). *Why primary sources*. Accessed at https://primarysources.icivics.org/why -primary-sources on April 24, 2023.

Investopedia Team. (2024, April 7). *What is a market economy and how does it work?* Accessed at https://investopedia.com/terms/m/marketeconomy.asp on April 15, 2024.

Johnson & Johnson. (1931, October 2). Stock your cabinet with reliable Johnson and Johnson products. *Evening Star*, C-7. Accessed at https://chroniclingamerica.loc.gov/lccn /sn83045462/1931-10-02/ed-1/seq-39 on August 13, 2024.

Johnson & Johnson. (1932, June 1). Johnson & Johnson first aid supplies. *Evening Star*, A-11. Accessed at https://chroniclingamerica.loc.gov/lccn/sn83045462/1932-06-01/ed-1 /seq-11 on August 13, 2024.

Johnson & Johnson. (1940, January 21). [Advertisement for Band-Aid adhesive bandages]. *Evening Star*, 8. Accessed at https://chroniclingamerica.loc.gov/lccn/sn83045462/1940-01 -21/ed-1/seq-100 on August 13, 2024.

Kagan, J. (2024, March 10). *The greatest generation: Definition and characteristics*. Accessed at https://investopedia.com/terms/t/the_greatest_generation.asp on April 15, 2024.

Kagan, S. (1994). *Cooperative learning* (Rev. ed.). San Clemente, CA: Author.

Kansas State Department of Education. (n.d.). *History, government and social studies (HGSS)*. Accessed at www.ksde.org/Agency/Division-of-Learning-Services/Career-Standards -and-Assessment-Services/Content-Area-F-L/History-Government-and-Social-Studies on March 25, 2023.

Kansas State Department of Education. (2023, September 14). *History, government and social studies: Elementary school rubric*. Accessed at www.ksde.org/LinkClick.aspx?file ticket=6mNTA9nfRlY%3D&tabid=472&portalid=0&mid=5612 on April 15, 2024.

Klassen, J. (2012). *This is not my hat*. Somerville, MA: Candlewick Press.

Levinson, M., & Levine, P. (2013). Taking informed action to engage students in civic life. *Social Education, 77*(6), 339–341.

Lewkowicz, J., & Leung, C. (2021). Classroom-based assessment. *Language Teaching, 54*(1), 47–57.

Liben, M., & Pimentel, S. (n.d.). *Placing text at the center of the standards-aligned ELA classroom*. New York: Achieve the Core. Accessed at https://achievethecore.org/content /upload/Text-at-the-Center-Report-V5.pdf on June 9, 2023.

Library of Congress. (n.d.a). *Chronicling America: Historic American newspapers—Le Meschacébé. [volume], November 06, 1885*. Accessed at https://chroniclingamerica.loc.gov /lccn/sn86079080/1885-11-06/ed-1/seq-4 on March 21, 2024.

Library of Congress. (n.d.b). *Getting started with primary sources*. Accessed at www.loc .gov/programs/teachers/getting-started-with-primary-sources on March 13, 2023.

Library of Congress (n.d.c). *Primary source sets*. Accessed at www.loc.gov/programs/teachers /classroom-materials/primary-source-sets on August 2, 2024.

Library of Congress. (n.d.d). *Zoom in Colorado–Buffalo Bill*. Accessed at https://docs.google .com/presentation/d/1Iv47vmm6Oi_DUwkrb6atkfyMDN70_kJpHx2V-cR0a9M/ edit#slide=id.p11 on March 25, 2023.

Library of Congress. (n.d.e.) *Primary source analysis tool*. Washington, DC: Author. Accessed at www.loc.gov/static/programs/teachers/getting-started-with-primary-sources/documents /Primary_Source_Analysis_Tool_LOC.pdf on August 2, 2024.

Libresco, A. S., & Balantic, J. (2013, September/October). Our conversation with you about "Effectively integrating literature and social studies . . ." *Social Studies and the Young Learner, 26*(1), 1, 4.

Lyman, F. (1981). The responsive classroom discussion: The inclusion of all students. In A. S. Anderson (Ed.), *Mainstreaming Digest: A Collection of Faculty and Student Papers* (pp. 109–113). College Park, MD: University of Maryland.

McLeod, S., & Shareski, D. (2018). *Different schools for a different world.* Bloomington, IN: Solution Tree Press.

McTighe, J. (2019a, August 28). Back-to-school lessons from an education giant. *Educational Leadership, 77*(1).

McTighe, J. (2019b, September 1). The fundamentals of backward planning. *Educational Leadership, 77*(1).

McTighe, J., & Wiggins, G. (2012). *From Common Core standards to curriculum: Five big ideas.* Accessed at https://grantwiggins.files.wordpress.com/2012/09/mctighe_wiggins _final_common_core_standards.pdf on September 16, 2023.

McTighe, J., & Wiggins, G. (2013). *Essential questions: Opening doors to student understanding.* Arlington, VA: ASCD.

Mehta, J., & Fine, S. (2019). *In search of deeper learning: The quest to remake the American high school.* Cambridge, MA: Harvard University Press.

Michigan Department of Education. (n.d.). *Michigan K–12 social studies standards.* Accessed at https://michigan.gov/-/media/Project/Websites/mde/Academic-Standards/Social_Studies _Standards.pdf?rev=4bab170dd4114e2dbce578723b37ca63 on September 16, 2023.

Minero, E. (2015, December 15). *Integrating subjects in elementary school.* Accessed at https://edutopia.org/practice/departmentalization-and-integration-deeper-learning -elementary-students on May 7, 2023.

Missouri State Department of Elementary and Secondary Education, Council of Chief State School Officers, & ACT. (2001, September). *The comprehensive social studies assessment project (CSSAP) professional development manual.* Accessed at https://eric.ed.gov/?id=ED474133 on September 23, 2023.

Monte-Sano, C. (2018). *Writing to learn history: Annotations and mini-writes.* Accessed at https://teachinghistory.org/teaching-materials/teaching-guides/23554 on April 23, 2023.

National Archives. (n.d.) *Analyze a photograph.* Washington, DC: Author. Accessed at www. archives.gov/files/education/lessons/document-analysis/english/analyze-a -photograph-novice.pdf on August 19, 2024.

National Center for Education Statistics. (n.d.). *An overview of NAEP.* Accessed at https://nces.ed.gov/nationsreportcard/subject/about/pdf/naep_overview_brochure_2018.pdf on August 27, 2023.

National Council for the Social Studies. (n.d.a). *About National Council for the Social Studies.* Accessed at https://socialstudies.org/about on March 13, 2023.

National Council for the Social Studies. (n.d.b). *National curriculum standards for social studies: Chapter 2—The themes of social studies.* Accessed at https://socialstudies.org /national-curriculum-standards-social-studies-chapter-2-themes-social-studies on September 22, 2023.

National Council for the Social Studies. (2013). *College, career, and civic life (C3) framework for social studies state standards: Guidance for enhancing the rigor of K–12 civics, economics, geography, and history.* Silver Spring, MD: Author. Accessed at https://socialstudies.org /system/files/2022/c3-framework-for-social-studies-rev0617.2.pdf on March 13, 2023.

National Council for the Social Studies. (2016). *Powerful, purposeful pedagogy in elementary school social studies* [Position statement]. Accessed at https://socialstudies.org/position -statements/powerful-purposeful-pedagogy-elementary-school-social-studies on May 14, 2023.

National Governors Association Center for Best Practices, & Council of Chief State School Officers. (2010). *Common Core State Standards for English language arts and literacy in history/social studies, science, and technical subjects.* Washington, DC: Authors. Accessed at https://learning.ccsso.org/wp-content/uploads/2022/11/ADA-Compliant-ELA-Standards .pdf on April 15, 2024.

Naylor, P. R. (2000). *Shiloh.* New York: Atheneum Books for Young Readers.

Ness, M. (2024). *Read alouds for all learners: A comprehensive plan for every subject, every day, grades K–8.* Bloomington, IN: Solution Tree Press.

Nickelsen, L., & Dickson, M. (2019). *Teaching with the instructional cha-chas: 4 steps to make learning stick.* Bloomington, IN: Solution Tree Press.

Nickelsen, L., & Dickson, M. (2022). *The literacy triangle: 50+ high-impact strategies to integrate reading, discussing, and writing in K–8 classrooms.* Bloomington, IN: Solution Tree Press.

North Carolina Department of Public Instruction. (2012, February 24). *Instructional support tools for achieving new standards.* Accessed at www.halifax.k12.nc.us/cms/lib/NC0221 4542/Centricity/Domain/336/5th%20Grade%20Social%20Studies%20Unpacking%20 Guide.pdf on March 25, 2023.

Novak, S., & Slattery, C. (2017). *Deep discourse: A framework for cultivating student-led discussions.* Bloomington, IN: Solution Tree Press.

Oakhill, J., Cain, K., & Elbro, C. (2015). *Understanding and teaching reading comprehension: A handbook.* New York: Routledge.

Ontario Curriculum. (2013). *Social studies: Grades 1 to 6; History and geography: Grades 7 and 8.* Accessed at www.edu.gov.on.ca/eng/curriculum/elementary/sshg18curr2013.pdf on September 16, 2023.

Oxford University Press. (n.d.). *Oxford Dictionary of Literary Terms:* close reading. Accessed at www.oxfordreference.com/display/10.1093/acref/9780198715443.001.0001/acref-978 0198715443-e-1242?rskey=pBpySx&result=1 on August 27, 2024.

Pandolpho, B. (2020). *I'm listening: How teacher-student relationships improve reading, writing, speaking, and listening.* Bloomington, IN: Solution Tree Press.

Pfundstein, V. (2012). *Veterans: Heroes in our neighborhood* (A. Anderson, Illus.). Deer Park, NY: Pfun-Omenal Stories.

Pinborough, J. (2013). *Miss Moore thought otherwise: How Anne Carroll Moore created libraries for children* (D. Atwell, Illus.). New York: Houghton Mifflin Harcourt.

Pondiscio, R. (2023, April 13). *At long last, E.D. Hirsch, Jr. gets his due: New research shows big benefits from core knowledge.* Accessed at https://fordhaminstitute.org/national/commentary/long-last-ed-hirsch-jr-gets-his-due-new-research-shows-big-benefits-core on April 18, 2023.

Potash, B. (2020, September 11). *Hexagonal thinking: A colorful tool for discussion.* Accessed at www.cultofpedagogy.com/hexagonal-thinking on June 21, 2023.

Primary source. (n.d.). In *Merriam-Webster's online dictionary.* Accessed at https://merriam-webster.com/dictionary/primary%20source on March 12, 2024.

Project Zero. (2019). *Word-phrase-sentence.* Cambridge, MA: Harvard Graduate School of Education. Accessed at https://pz.harvard.edu/sites/default/files/Word-Phrase-Sentence.pdf on April 15, 2024.

Project Zero. (2022). *Project Zero's thinking routine toolbox.* Cambridge, MA: Harvard Graduate School of Education. Accessed at www.pz.harvard.edu/thinking-routines on March 14, 2023.

Rasinski, T. V. (2012). Why reading fluency should be hot! *The Reading Teacher,* 65(8), 516–522.

Reading Rockets. (n.d.). *Classroom strategies: Inferencing.* Accessed at https://readingrockets.org/classroom/classroom-strategies/inferencing on October 31, 2023.

ReadWorks. (n.d.a). *Who is a good citizen at school?* Accessed at www.readworks.org/article/Community-Life/085bb0dc-6609-41e7-92e2-43a4c6185bf9#!articleTab:content/contentSection:d53a36e0-d740-4321-b6a8-1bb466e03b78 on August 13, 2024.

ReadWorks. (n.d.b). *Why do we need rules?* Accessed at www.readworks.org/article/Community-Life/085bb0dc-6609-41e7-92e2-43a4c6185bf9#!articleTab:content/contentSection:39180fc3-9d95-44e7-b220-9383a0634130 on August 13, 2024.

Reed, D., & Parhms, P. (n.d.). *Delivering explicit vocabulary instruction: Using the Frayer model* [Blog post]. Accessed at https://greatmiddleschools.org/delivering-explicit-vocabulary-instruction-using-the-frayer-model on May 7, 2023.

Right Question Institute. (n.d.). *What is the QFT?* Accessed at https://rightquestion.org/what-is-the-qft on March 19, 2023.

Schmidt, J. (2022, March 19). *Disciplinary literacy in social studies* [Blog post]. Accessed at https://joeschmidtsocialstudies.com/blog/f/disciplinary-literacy-in-social-studies on January 16, 2024.

Schmidt, J., & Pinkney, N. (2022). *Civil discourse: Classroom conversations for stronger communities.* Thousand Oaks, CA: Corwin Press.

Schwartz, S. (2023). *Using a curriculum rich in arts, history, and science led to big reading improvements.* Accessed at https://edweek.org/teaching-learning/using-a-curriculum-rich-in-arts-history-and-science-led-to-big-reading-improvements/2023/04 on May 14, 2023.

Shanahan, T. (2012, June 18). *What is close reading?* [Blog post]. Accessed at https://shanahanonliteracy.com/blog/what-is-close-reading on October 28, 2023.

Shanahan, T. (2013, November 19). *The close reading of historical documents* [Blog post]. Accessed at www.shanahanonliteracy.com/blog/the-close-reading-of-historical-documents on June 28, 2024.

Shanahan, T. (2017, March 17). *Disciplinary literacy: The basics* [Blog post]. Accessed at https://shanahanonliteracy.com/blog/disciplinary-literacy-the-basics on December 23, 2023.

Shannon, D. (1999). *David goes to school.* New York: Blue Sky Press.

Sherriff, L. (2016). *Why beavers were parachuted into the Idaho wilderness 73 years ago.* Accessed at www.nationalgeographic.com/animals/article/why-beavers-were-parachuted -into-the-idaho-wilderness on August 6, 2024.

Snyder, R. C. (2016). *What is a veteran, anyway?* (R. Himler, Illus.). West Bay Shore, NY: Blue Marlin.

Stanford University. (n.d.). *Why study history?* Accessed at https://history.stanford.edu /academics/why-study-history on January 16, 2024.

Swan, K., Lee, J. K., & Grant, S. G. (2018). *Inquiry design model: Building inquiries in social studies.* Silver Spring, MD: National Council for the Social Studies.

Teachinghistory.org. (n.d.). *HSI: Historical scene investigation.* Accessed at https://teaching history.org/history-content/website-reviews/24983 on March 12, 2024.

TeachingWorks Research Library. (n.d.). *Setting up and managing small group work.* Accessed at https://library.teachingworks.org/curriculum-resources/materials/social-studies-setting -up-and-managing-small-group-work on June 29, 2024.

Textproject.org. (n.d.a). *FYI for kids! Volume 1, issue 1.* Accessed at https://textproject.org/wp -content/uploads/fyi4k/FYI-for-Kids-Level-1-ALL.pdf on August 6, 2024.

Textproject.org. (n.d.b). *Playing by the rules.* Accessed at https://textproject.org/wp-content /uploads/fyi4k/FYI-for-Kids-4-15-play-by-the-rules.pdf on August 13, 2024.

Textproject.org. (n.d.c). *A hero who gives things away.* Accessed at https://textproject.org/wp -content/uploads/fyi4k/FYI-for-Kids-1-15-A-hero-who-gives-things-away.pdf on August 13, 2024.

Textproject.org. (n.d.d) *Voting makes a difference.* Accessed at https://textproject.org/wp -content/uploads/fyi4k/FYI-for-Kids-1-10-Voting-makes-a-difference.pdf on August 13, 2024.

Tyner, A., & Kabourek, S. (2020). *Social studies instruction and reading comprehension: Evidence from the early childhood longitudinal study.* Washington, DC: Thomas B. Fordham Institute. Accessed at https://fordhaminstitute.org/national/resources/social-studies -instruction-and-reading-comprehension on April 18. 2023.

Visible Learning. (n.d.). *Hattie ranking: 252 influences and effect sizes related to student achievement.* Accessed at https://visible-learning.org/hattie-ranking-influences-effect-sizes -learning-achievement on September 17, 2023.

Waring, S. M. (Ed.). (2023). *Using inquiry to prepare students for college, career, and civic life (elementary grades)*. Silver Spring, MD: National Council for the Social Studies. Accessed at https://ebooks.socialstudies.org/downloads/tps-elementary/Using_Inquiry_to_Prepare _Students_for_College_Career_and_Civic_Life-Elementary_Grades.pdf on May 6, 2024.

Wellman, B., & Lipton, L. (2017). *Data-driven dialogue: A facilitator's guide to collaborative inquiry* (2nd ed.). Arlington, MA: Mira Via, LLC.

Wesson, S. (2011a, June 28). *Look again: Challenging students to develop close observation skills* [Blog post]. Accessed at https://blogs.loc.gov/teachers/2011/06/look-again-challenging -students-to-develop-close-observation-skills/?loclr=blogtea on April 30, 2023.

Wesson, S. (2011b, September 27). *Looking harder: Inspiring close observation* [Blog post]. Accessed at https://blogs.loc.gov/teachers/2011/09/looking-harder-inspiring-close -observation/?loclr=blogtea on October 31, 2023.

Wexler, N. (2019). *The knowledge gap: The hidden cause of America's broken education system— And how to fix it*. New York: Avery.

Wexler, N. (2024). Foreword. In M. Ness, *Read alouds for all learners: A comprehensive plan for every subject, every day, grades K–8* (pp. ix–xii). Bloomington, IN: Solution Tree Press.

Wiggins, G. (2014, December 8). *Questions about questions: NCSS and UbD*. Accessed at https://authenticeducation.org/questions-about-questions-ncss-and-ubd on September 17, 2023.

Wiggins, G. (2015). How to make your questions essential. *Educational Leadership*, *73*(1), 10–15.

Wittenstein, B. (2018). *The boo-boos that changed the world: A true story about an accidental invention (really!)* (C. Hsu, Illus.). Watertown, MA: Charlesbridge.

Wood, S. (2017). *The skydiving beavers: A true tale* (G. van Frankenhuyzen, Illus.). Ann Arbor, MI: Sleeping Bear Press.

Wright, T. S. (2021). *A teacher's guide to vocabulary development across the day*. Portsmouth, NH: Heinemann.

Index

The Digital Projects Playbook
John Arthur
Students in today's classrooms live in a digital world. Tap into the unique opportunities this offers with author John Arthur's collection of resource-packed projects designed to leverage students' digital skills and support their academic, cognitive, and creative development.
BKG171

Rigor Redefined
Michael McDowell
Teachers can use Michael McDowell's 10 learning habits, practical tools, and templates to actualize rigorous instruction in short and sharp ways that drive student learning and create a lasting impact. Discover how to connect the dots between surface, deep, and transfer learning.
BKG193

Read Alouds for All Learners
Molly Ness
In *Read Alouds for All Learners: A Comprehensive Plan for Every Subject, Every Day, Grades PreK–8*, Molly Ness provides a compelling case for the integration, or reintegration, of the read aloud in schools and a step-by-step resource for preK–8 educators in classrooms.
BKG116

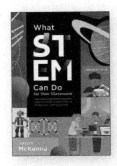

What STEM Can Do for Your Classroom
Jason McKenna
Author and educator Jason McKenna offers examples, tried and tested classroom projects, and collaborative strategies in this innovative resource designed to open up STEM education for K–6 educators in exciting and expansive new ways.
BKG088

Solution Tree | Press
a division of

Solution Tree

Visit SolutionTree.com or call 800.733.6786 to order.